OTHELLO

LOVING NOT WISELY BUT TOO WELL

The Tragedy of Specialness

OTHELLO

LOVING NOT WISELY BUT TOO WELL

The Tragedy of Specialness

KENNETH WAPNICK, Ph.D.

Foundation for A COURSE IN MIRACLES®

Foundation for A COURSE IN MIRACLES®
41397 Buecking Drive
Temecula, CA 92590
www.facim.org

Copyright 2004 by the
Foundation for A COURSE IN MIRACLES®

Printed in China

CONTENTS

INTRODUCTION 1

CHAPTER 1   Special Relationships 3

CHAPTER 2   *Othello*: The Play and the Characters 19
             What Motivates Iago? 22
             Verdi's *Otello*: Iago's Credo 28
             Why Did Othello Listen to Iago? 34

CHAPTER 3   *A Course in Miracles*: Othello and the Ego 41
             Asking God for Special Favor 41
             Silencing the Voice of the Holy Spirit 51
             Asking for Specifics 59
             Guilt Demands Punishment – Self-Sabotage 63

CHAPTER 4   Jesus: Teaching with Gentle Means and Easy Tasks 71

CLOSING MEDITATION
             Choose Once Again 81

APPENDIX   Iago's Credo 84
             A Course in Miracles 85

INDEX OF REFERENCES TO *A COURSE IN MIRACLES* 87

Foundation for A COURSE IN MIRACLES® 89

INTRODUCTION[1]

The title for this last in the series of four volumes on Shakespeare's great tragedies and *A Course in Miracles* is borrowed from a line near the end of *Othello* when, after killing his wife Desdemona, and just before killing himself, Othello asks the people around him when they tell his story to speak *"of one that loved not wisely, but too well"* (V,ii,345).[2] That thought constitutes the sub-theme for our discussion of special relationships, and I will use the character of Othello to illustrate this major theme of *A Course in Miracles*. Our major focus thus will be on the meaning of specialness, the guilt that inevitably follows from its pursuit, and the fact that once we feel guilty we condemn ourselves to a life of failure, pain, loss, and self-sabotage as punishment for our choice to be special.

The book is divided into four parts. First, I discuss special relationships in terms of its ontology and the ensuing guilt, and then how we live out the thought system of specialness in our everyday lives. In the second part, I talk about Shakespeare's play, and use it as a means of illustrating what I have already presented. The third part consists of my reading various passages from *A Course in Miracles,* which will allow us to review the dynamics of specialness and the process of releasing ourselves from the grasp of that insidious thought system. I conclude by discussing the gentle role of our teacher Jesus, who helps us end the nightmare world of guilt and death by releasing us from the grip of specialness through forgiveness. A meditation on passages from the final section of the text closes the book.

---

1. A general introduction to this four-volume series on the great tragedies of Shakespeare appears in the Introduction in Volume I, *King Lear - Love and Be Silent.*
2. All Shakespeare quotations are from: *William Shakespeare • The Complete Works •* The Edition of the Shakespeare Head Press, Oxford (New York: Dorset Press, 1988). Line numbers cited refer to the first line quoted.

Chapter 1

SPECIAL RELATIONSHIPS

Anyone who has worked with *A Course in Miracles* for a while would almost certainly acknowledge that the subject of special relationships is by far the most difficult in the Course, not only in understanding, but even more so in accepting how this thought system—infused with hate, murder, betrayal, and guilt—permeates just about every aspect of our lives. In fact, I would even state that students could not claim to be serious about *A Course in Miracles* without having carefully and honestly addressed this issue, spending considerable time focusing on how specialness actually plays out in their lives. The consequences of not recognizing our investment in specialness are terrible. One of the reasons Shakespeare's plays have captivated people across centuries is that they are not simply dramas about fictional characters, but about people with whom it is very difficult *not* to identify. This should become clearer when we come to discuss the play itself.

Let us start at the beginning. When I talk about the birth of the ego thought system and its development, I usually begin with the "tiny, mad idea" and this familiar passage: "Into eternity, where all is one, there crept a tiny, mad idea, at which the Son of God remembered not to laugh" (T-27.VIII.6:2). Here is the beginning—or seeming beginning—of the miserable mess that is the world, and there are many ways of speaking about it. Since the tiny, mad idea never really happened, anything we say about it is made up. From one point of view, this *make-believe* can be thought of as myth; and *A Course in Miracles*, like so many other cultural expressions throughout history, has a mythology. It begins with Heaven, the state of perfect Oneness, followed by our descent once we made the choice for the ego—the infamous "tiny, mad idea."

I will be discussing the tiny, mad idea and its aftermath from the perspective of specialness. We will later read a passage from the text that explicitly states that the separation began when we demanded special favor from God. When He did not grant it, we made Him into an unloving Father. In the Heavenly state of perfect Oneness—the state of reality and our true Self—there is no separation or differentiation, only the perfect oneness of love, the nature of God. In Heaven, therefore, there are

3

no separate beings—no differentiated Creator *and* created, Father and Son, God and Christ, Cause and Effect. Only One. Words are inevitably set within a dualistic framework; symbolic expressions of the mythology. But true reality is beyond all words, symbols, and myths. In the state of Oneness there is no otherness; no separate beings that can relate to each other, let alone notice the other.

And so, into the eternal state of Oneness there crept this impossible idea. It is impossible because it could not have happened in the reality of perfect Oneness; therefore, it did not happen. Yet it *seems* to have happened, and our lives on earth witness to the fact that we indeed pulled off the impossible, separating from our Creator and Source. In the instant we seemed to separate, the Son of God became conscious and perceived himself in relationship to God. He saw himself as a distinct being, independent of, and separate from his Creator; and he wanted God to notice him. Needless to say, God could not because there was nothing to notice. There was no separate Son; no separate self— there was nothing. The ego thought system actually begins at this point.

Our mythology grows in appeal because of the separated Son's response to God's non-response to his request for attention, or special favor. From God's point of view, there could be no special favor because there is only perfect Oneness. Thus God does nothing, says nothing; indeed, He does not even hear the request. How could He know about what never happened? But we—the one Son of God—by experiencing ourselves as separate, heard the request we made, and demanded that God experience us in the same way. To this day, we keep asking God to notice us, pay attention to our needs, acknowledge our existence, call us by name; even yell and scream if He must, but at least to pay attention to us. Yet from the very beginning His response has been absolutely nothing. With no other option available to our separated minds, we took matters into our own hands and in effect said to our Source: "If You will not grant us our specialness, or provide the attention we crave, You leave us no choice but to make up a world in which we *will* be noticed. If You will not give us the love, devotion, kindness, and respect we deserve, we will leave You and find them elsewhere. If you will not acknowledge this independent entity we now call our self, we will find someone who will." Again, these words are but symbolic expressions of a phenomenon that cannot be described in any other way but the language of myth.

Once we took the tiny, mad idea seriously and demanded special favor, separation from God became a reality and we sought to protect our specialness—the separate, unique, individual, autonomous entity we think of as our self. And all the while God knows absolutely nothing about us, which infuriates us even more. You may recall "The Little Garden," where Jesus speaks of an infinitesimal ripple on the ocean that thinks it is the ocean, and a sunbeam that thinks it is the sun:

> The body is a tiny fence around a little part of a glorious and complete idea. It draws a circle, infinitely small, around a very little segment of Heaven, splintered from the whole, proclaiming that within it is your kingdom, where God can enter not.
> Within this kingdom the ego rules, and cruelly. And to defend this little speck of dust it bids you fight against the universe. This fragment of your mind is such a tiny part of it that, could you but appreciate the whole, you would see instantly that it is like the smallest sunbeam to the sun, or like the faintest ripple on the surface of the ocean. In its amazing arrogance, this tiny sunbeam has decided it is the sun; this almost imperceptible ripple hails itself as the ocean (T-18.VIII.2:5-3:4).

The sun and ocean know nothing of these fantasies—"Yet neither sun nor ocean is even aware of all this strange and meaningless activity" (T-18.VIII.4:1). Likewise, the ego's fantasy of a separate self, inhabiting a body and living in a world, is played out within a mind that has become delusional, wherein the Son of God believes he is separate and on his own; basically having answered his own request for special favor and attention. God did not grant his demand, and so the Son granted it to himself, essentially telling God to get lost: "I do not need You—Your Kingdom, Love, or perfect Oneness. I have taken matters into my own hands, giving myself what You denied me. Look! I now exist as a separate entity and creator in my own right."

It is clear from this that in the instant we limited our understanding of the awareness of love, we changed its definition to special love. It evolved into what here on earth exists between two people. This holds not only for romantic or sexual love, but *all* love: between parent and child, friends, us and God, and us and Jesus. Everything we call love occurs between two or more separate individuals. It applies as well to loving ourselves, for when I exhibit self-love, I take care of myself and treat myself well. However, there is always a sense of an *I* that is taking care of this other *I*, which is also a separated self. All special love reflects this duality: differentiation and separation. This is the exact opposite of the true meaning of love—in fact, it is the *denial* of love. An important section—"The Choice for Completion" (T-16.V)—contrasts the ego's view of completion with the Holy Spirit's. In the former we complete ourselves by joining with someone or something else perceived to be external; in the latter we are *already* complete within ourselves, which we come to understand when we choose to listen to God's Voice. This true completion is our Self as Christ, totally at one with God.

Many readers will recall that early in the text Jesus makes a distinction between *being* and *existence* (T-4.VII.5). *Being* is associated with spirit, God, and truth. *Existence* is associated with the ego and separation. In the *un*holy instant when we believed the tiny, mad idea and made its specialness real, we denied our being as spirit and Christ, and affirmed our existence as a separated self or, most importantly for our discussion here, a *special* self. The Being of God was denied so that we could exist, and that became the first statement of the reigning principle of the ego thought system: *one or the other.* If I am to exist—to have the specialness I need, crave, and covet—someone will have to be sacrificed. If I am to win my specialness, someone will have to lose. Since at the beginning there are only two characters in the ego's cosmic drama, and since in the ego's script the Son wins a separate existence, God had to be sacrificed. It became a matter of *one or the other.* I now exist supreme and *being* has been sacrificed, falling into non-existence. God's Love, which is all-inclusive within Himself, cannot co-exist with special love, which is exclusive and differentiated. That is the meaning of the term *special—one or the other.* There is a winner and loser: being *or* existence; totality *or* separation; Oneness *or* differences.

The choice we made at the beginning was to follow the ego and turn our backs on God. In the context of Othello's self-assessment, "*one that loved not wisely, but too well*" (V,ii,345), we can say that our choice to love the ego instead of God was not a wise one. But once we chose the separated self, we loved that self too well. Thus—we "*loved not wisely, but too well.*" The effect of that choice was the sacrifice of God, because love and specialness cannot coexist. In making the decision to turn away from God and His Love, we essentially said: "I do not want to disappear into the Heart of God and become part of indivisible being. I want to be a differentiated and special self; I want to be me, to count for something, to be noticed. I want attention!" From that point on, from the ego's perspective, it did not matter whether someone paid attention by yelling, screaming, and finding fault, or by being devoted. Either way, the ego now counts for something. The true God, of course, did none of those things. Not knowing about the separation, God could not notice it. Since it could not have happened, *it did not happen.*

Once we decided against God and for the ego, we slipped into the unreal state *A Course in Miracles* refers to as a dream of separation. The Son could not have his specialness in reality, but in dreams. When we fell asleep, we took with us into this dream a memory of Whom we had chosen against, for choosing for the ego is to choose against God. In effect, we gave God a chance and from our point of view He blew it. Therefore, we fired Him as our Creator. In essence, we destroyed Him and on His slain corpse built our own self. Nonetheless, we carry this memory of God and His Love with us, referred to in the Course as the Holy Spirit.

As the memory of reality, the Holy Spirit is the mind's Voice that speaks of our innocence and love. That is the Voice to which we originally chose not to listen, and which we continue to reject. Since it is now *one or the other* that governs our existence, if we listen to God's Voice we will no longer believe the ego's voice, which speaks to us of our special and unique self. The Holy Spirit reminds us of what *A Course in Miracles* calls the *principle of the Atonement*: separation is impossible; therefore we never left God and remain an indivisible part of His Being. We never separated from reality; we just believed we did. Thus if we listen to the Voice of the Atonement, our individual existence disappears. Yet if we continue to listen to the ego, the Voice of the Atonement disappears. Once we decide for the ego we *become* the ego, and the Holy Spirit and our Self are forgotten.

Remember that the ego—the individual and special self we have chosen—is not a separate entity acting on its own; not a thought system separate from, and outside our minds. *The ego is us*, once we have chosen to believe we are separated. We speak of it as something separate because that makes it easier to talk about. It also highlights the idea that we can choose between two thought systems: the ego's and the Holy Spirit's. But, again, when we choose the ego, for all intents and purposes we *become* the ego.

The part of our minds that has chosen the ego recognizes there is a great threat looming on the horizon: what might happen if we change our minds? Thus, if I were to recognize that the ego has lied to me, what happens if I decide to choose against it and for the Holy Spirit? What happens if I recognize that He speaks the truth and I now choose to listen to Him? The answer is clear: This special and unique self will disappear; the "I" with whom I identify will cease to exist.

Of crucial importance here—and we will see this again when we discuss *Othello*—is understanding that the ego has no issue with God or the Holy Spirit. It does not understand Them, nor even know about Their existence. The ego's problem is with the part of our minds that can choose, what we refer to as the decision maker. If left to itself, the decision maker would quickly recognize that the ego made all this up, was not an honest broker, and therefore not to be trusted. We would thus change our minds and choose against the ego, thereby extinguishing it. The ego, then, fears and hates that decision-making part of our minds, recognizing that having first chosen for specialness and against love, it can just as easily choose for love and against specialness. Our capacity to choose is thus the ego's major concern. Further, if the ego is extinguished in our minds by our choosing against it, the self that identifies with the ego is extinguished as well.

The ego thus comes up with a strategy for seeing to it that the Son of God never changes his mind; a brilliant strategy that makes the ego's myth so interesting and compelling. The ego recognizes that the only way it can be safe is to ensure that the separated self—the Son of God in his dream of separation—never changes his mind. The goal of the ego's strategy is therefore to render the Son mindless; if he does not know he has a mind, how can he possibly change it? If we cannot change our minds, the original decision for the ego will stand forever. Thus, too, will specialness reign forever and the Love of God rendered non-existent. And all that need happen for the ego's triumph to be complete is for the Son of God to be unaware he has a mind.

This is where the ego begins to develop *its* myth—a myth within the larger myth of separation. To fulfill its goal, the ego tells the Son a tale whose sole purpose is to have him shift to a permanent state of mindlessness. In an important section called "Setting the Goal," Jesus explains that we always set the goal first (T-17.VI). Once we understand our goal, we will understand how all situations—everything occurring in any given day—are the purposive means of achieving it. If we lack this understanding we will not perceive the meaning of anything in our lives. While the ego's thought system—the capstone of which is mindlessness—is totally insane, it is nonetheless perfectly logical and consistent—brilliantly conceived, orchestrated, and performed.

And so the ego makes up a story it believes will so frighten the Son of God that he will voluntarily, and with great eagerness choose to leave his mind, believing it to be a most dangerous place. This story has three foundation stones: *sin, guilt,* and *fear.* The ego convinces the Son that his leaving God is a *sin*; a sin so horrendous that he is overwhelmed with *guilt,* deserving punishment for what he has done. The Son thus must *fear* the punishment the ego has convinced him is inevitable and justifiably forthcoming. In its tale the ego tells the Son: "Yes, you now exist; yes, you are special and unique; and yes, it is true that God should have paid attention to you and did not. But did you really have to do what you did—*kill* Him?"

Keep in mind—and this will become important when we discuss *Othello*—that once the Son has silenced the Holy Spirit by choosing the ego, the principle of *one or the other* dictates that the Holy Spirit cannot be heard. Thus there is no longer a Voice we hear that speaks the truth, for all that remains are the sounds of the ego, its voice telling us anything that serves its purpose of separation and mindlessness. Because there is no other voice to which to compare it, what the "honest" ego tells the Son is accepted as true. Since there is no alternative and the Son has completely negated the Voice of the Holy Spirit, to him the ego essentially becomes God's voice.

With no truth as comparison, the ego's story is bought hook, line, and sinker. It says: "Everything you have thought and done is true, but why did you act so precipitously and violently? Did you have to destroy love simply to meet your needs? There must have been some other way you could have gotten what you wanted." The ego naturally never told the Son this "other way," and he never suspects the ego's lies. It simply weaved its web of deceit, which was truth to the Son. The ego continues: "You have done an horrendous thing, committed an egregious sin, a heinous crime beyond words—the destruction of perfect Love." The Son listens, overwhelmed with shame, guilt, and grief at his crime. The ego says further: "The stain of God's blood is on your hands and you will never wash it away," similar to Lady Macbeth's experience. And if the overwhelming guilt were not enough, to make things even worse the ego adds: "Your sin has won you a mortal enemy. God will rise out of the grave of your specialness and punish you."

9

Remember, the ego can say anything it wants and make it true. Thus one minute God is dead, and the next He is emerging out of the grave, just as in any horror movie. The ego tells the Son that God is coming after him to take back the life he stole from Him. Since it is *one or the other*, if the Son has life and God does not, He is dead; but if God takes life back, the Son will die. And the ego adds ominously: "*You* will not rise from the grave because God will not make the mistake you did. When He kills you, you remain dead. Finally, there is a hell to which He will assign you after your demise. Listen carefully and you will hear His footsteps. He has found you and is entering your mind, even as we speak." At this point in the story the mind is the only place that exists, and the Son appears doomed: He has sinned and is to be punished for it. Since his sin took life, his punishment is the removal of that same life: an eye for an eye; a life for a life. His existence will come to an end, almost as quickly as it seemed to begin.

As per the ego's plan, the Son is panicked by the story. His grief, guilt, and self-hatred are cast aside, leaving only the terror that he will be destroyed if he remains one instant longer in the mind—a battle-ground on which he is pitted against God. The Son screams to the ego in desperation: "Do something!" to which the ego replies: "I have a plan. There is a way to escape the battleground." The Son pleads, "Any-thing! I will do anything, but don't hesitate; those footsteps are getting closer." There are, of course, no footsteps, but guilt generates fearful tales: we believe people say things they are not saying; thinking and doing things they are not thinking or doing. *A Course in Miracles* says guilt is blind and is blinding (T-13.IX.7-8). It is blind because it does not see the truth, and blinding because it does not let us see the truth. Guilt cancels everything out except what it wants us to perceive: the threat of imminent punishment.

The ego now has the Son right where it wants him. It needed him to be motivated to leave his mind, which is why it made up its nightmare tale of sin, guilt, and fear, which culminated in the belief he is about to be destroyed. And so the ego says to the terror-stricken Son: "Take my hand and we will be gone. We will leave the mind and God will never know our whereabouts."

The dynamic of "leaving the mind" is *projection*, wherein some-thing you judge to be unacceptable in your mind—the guilt that leads to fear of punishment—is placed outside it, enabling you magically to believe it is gone. On the macrocosmic level, projection is the Course's explanation of the origin of the physical universe; its version of the "Big Bang." As Jesus explains at the beginning of Chapter 18:

> ...nothing you have seen begins to show you the enormity of the original error, which seemed to cast you out of Heaven, to shatter knowledge into meaningless bits of disunited perceptions, and to force you to make further substitutions.
> That was the first projection of error outward. The world arose to hide it, and became the screen on which it was projected and drawn between you and the truth (T-18.I.5:6-6:2).

Once the thought system of the ego was projected outside the mind—a thought system of separation, individuality, and specialness, now associated with sin, guilt, and fear—it gave rise to a world that perforce has the same characteristics. This brings us to another crucial principle in *A Course in Miracles*: *ideas leave not their source.* Ideas in our minds, despite the belief that we can get rid of them through projection, remain in our minds. The ideas of separation, specialness, guilt, fear of punishment, and death have never left their source in our minds; we just think they did. The ego's bread and butter is its own version of this principle: ideas *do* leave their source—what the ego tells us happened at the beginning. We were an idea in the Mind of God, our Source, and we did leave Him. The Holy Spirit's Atonement principle says: No, ideas do *not* leave their source. We are "at home in God, dreaming of exile" (T-10.I.2:1). Nothing has changed, for we are still part of perfect love. We just *think* something has happened to separate us from love, because we believe ideas leave their source.

That is how the ego was born, and how it protects itself from the threat that the mind will reverse its decision to identify with it. If the Son forgets he has a mind, as we have already seen, he cannot change his decision. Once the Son "leaves" his mind through projection, the ego causes a veil to fall between the mind and the Son's experience as a projected entity. That veil keeps him unaware of the world's origin. Moreover, once projected, the single thought of separation fragmented into billions and billions of pieces, and each one encased itself in a form we call the body. That is how a world of separate bodies came into existence. Since *ideas leave not their source*, every bodily-encased thought retains the entirety of the ego thought system, as well as the entirety of the Holy Spirit's corrective thought system of the Atonement.

11

Thus, we who walk this earth in seeming solitude (T-20.IV.5:3)—seemingly separated from each other—carry within the mind of which we are no longer aware, two thought systems we all share: the ego's thought system of specialness, and the Holy Spirit's of forgiveness. Most importantly, our split minds contain the power to choose between the two.

Some of you may remember that in my book *Love Does Not Condemn* I described the Gnosticism of Valentinus, arguably the greatest Gnostic teacher. The teachings of his school included a myth remarkably parallel to the one I just outlined.[3] It told the story of how the world was made, beginning when a part of God, called by the Gnostics *Sophia* (a feminine Greek word meaning "wisdom") decided she would create her own love and self, creating like her Father. Her problem was that she could not, because she was not God. Disaster inevitably followed, as she gave birth to an aborted fetus, the residue of which the Valentinians referred to as an abortion. This sent shock waves throughout Heaven, so God acted quickly to shield His creation from this aborted miscreation. The shield was called the Limit, similar to what the Course calls the Holy Spirit. You may recall that in *A Course in Miracles* Jesus tells us that God placed a limit on our ability to miscreate (T-2.III.3:3). That limit is the Holy Spirit, similar to this Gnostic notion of God's Limit, which prevented Sophia's abortion from getting back into Heaven. It also allowed its inhabitants to be held in ignorance of what was called Sophia's folly. Her abortion was then cast out of Heaven, existing outside as something separate. Sophia, aware of what she had done, was overwhelmed with grief, sadness, and fear, and also ignorance, because she did not know what was happening. While the Gnostics did not use the word *guilt*, Sophia's grief reaction is essentially the same, and so overwhelming that it took this aborted fetus, a thought form, and crystallized it into matter. From this arose the Demiurge—a term the Gnostics borrowed from their beloved Plato—which is the part of the separated self that made the universe. To most Gnostics, incidentally, this world was evil, having *not* been created by the true God.

One reason I wrote *Love Does Not Condemn* was to demonstrate the parallels and differences between Gnosticism and *A Course in*

3. *Love Does Not Condemn: The World, the Flesh, and the Devil According to Platonism, Christianity, Gnosticism, and A Course in Miracles*, pp. 151-57.

Miracles. One important parallel is the emphasis on guilt (or grief) as the problem. If we did not feel guilty about what we had done, nothing would have happened. In the Appendix I have included an excerpt from the Introduction to Chapter 13 in the text, which I will refer to more extensively later on, where Jesus describes the world as "the delusional system of those made mad by guilt" (T-13.in.2:2). Guilt is the problem. It is what made the world and sustains it. Above all, guilt is what sustains our special identity, for it prevents us from returning to the mind where guilt was conceived in the first place. Remember, when we projected ourselves and the world from the mind, the ego's veil of forgetfulness fell. This keeps us from the mind, so we retain no memory of where we or the world came from. All we know is that we are a self in a body. That unknowing self has all the thoughts and characteristics that were in the mind, because *ideas leave not their source*. That is why in so many places in *A Course in Miracles* Jesus tells us there is no world outside our thoughts.[4] The early workbook lessons, though not couched in metaphysical terms, express this point very clearly: The outer is determined by the inner; what we perceive outside comes from our minds' thoughts. The most profound of these thoughts is guilt over the specialness we believe we stole from Heaven, and the subsequent belief that Heaven will steal it back.

So here we are. We find ourselves born into a body, not as children of Heaven but of specialness. In the text Jesus speaks of specialness not only as our "son," but also our "father" (T-24.VII.10). Specialness conceived us, and it is specialness that we make into our reality as we forge more and more special relationships. Any time we believe we are happy in this world, or seem to get the love we want, there is guilt's little voice deep inside, which even though we do not know its source, yet we hear it. One way or another we hear the voice that says we do not deserve what we have. If we are a success, have love, health, money, and fame, guilt's nagging voice tells they are not really ours, for we attained them dishonestly. Indeed, we had to kill in order to get them, and therefore we do not deserve to keep them.

Knowing this helps us to understand why our lives are so filled with self-sabotage. In fact, the body was made to self-destruct, which it does by dying. Between birth and death the body is part of an ongoing process of self-destruction. It gets sick, and deteriorates as we get older,

---

4. See for example, T-21.in.1; W-pI.132.

failing more and more. Moreover, if it is not the "laws of nature" that do us in, others do so by assaulting us psychologically, and even physically. We are abused, victimized, and unfairly treated, guilt's voice reminding us: "You see? I told you so. You deserve none of this. The very fact you are born into a body proclaims that you stole life." That is why, when the ego made up its thought system and mythology, it included, above all, suffering and pain—physical and psychological. Consequently, the world, being "the delusional system of those made mad by guilt," is filled with suffering and pain, as that passage in the text explains (T-13.in.2).

A question remains: Why would we make such a world? Why would we not make a life that is wonderful, in which bodies are perfect and never break down or need anything, nor be in a perpetual state of lack? Why are bodies made to need other bodies? The answer lies in the ego's principle that guilt demands punishment. The law of specialness is that what you have, you stole, and therefore you deserve to have it stolen from you (T-23.II.13). That is why this world is not a happy place, but made to be its opposite. How could there be happiness when life here is built on God's corpse, continually nourished by His death, yet fearful of His reprisal? This insanity reflects the ego's fourth law of chaos: "You have what you have taken" (T-23.II.9). Again, if I have it, I took it; a sin for which I deserve to be punished.

Keep in mind that we are not talking about real love, which cannot be either stolen or lost. Love simply is, and there are no separate entities within it to be stolen from or to steal. To repeat: In the ego's version of love, to have it you must steal from another. That is how we came to be: stealing life from God, which did not come from us, but from Someone else. Therefore, being born states: I stole this life, and it is my just deserts to have it taken from me. That is why we made a world in which we have a body that dies. It does not matter whether it is called homo sapiens that dies in seventy years—sometimes sooner, sometimes later—or a rock that may take billions of years to decompose as it is inexorably pulverized by the elements. Everything in the universe deteriorates and comes to an end. Thus the ego can claim death as proof we deserve to be punished for our sin. But we never get in touch with this "sin" because it remains buried in our minds, accessed only through the Holy Spirit, and we buried Him and His Atonement thought at the beginning.

We therefore live lives of specialness, pain, and loss. Even when things work, we cannot help feeling guilty, even if the thought is unconscious. Self-sabotage is a factor in our lives in one way or another, but we blame our misbegotten fate on everyone and everything else: I lost money because of the stock market. I lost the love of my life because of cancer, or because he or she walked out on me. I lost my job because my boss is mean and unreasonable. I lost my job because *I* am mean and unreasonable, yet it was my parents' fault I turned out that way. We always have reasons for things happening the way they do. But we never look at the *real* reason, which is our decision for guilt that demands we be punished for our sin.

No one in this world escapes the laws of specialness—the ego's five laws of chaos (T-23.II). No one escapes them because they define our existence, and how and why we are here: the original thought of specialness—"God will not give me the love I want and deserve; therefore, I will get it on my own." Thus, again, we had to steal it from God, sacrificing our Creator for the special existence of independence. That is the truth behind our life here. Jesus is not making it up when he tells us: "You think you are the home of evil, darkness and sin" (W-pI.93.1:1). However deeply buried that self-concept might be, that *is* what we think. We are the ones who made this home, yet because the Voice of truth has been silenced we have forgotten. We accept the voice of the ego as truth's voice and listen to no other. Indeed, we do not know there is any other, for we are not even aware that we are listening to a voice. We have become that voice.

In "The Two Worlds" (T-18.IX.3-5) we find what is probably the clearest exposition in *A Course in Miracles* of the relationship between guilt and the body. Jesus explains that the body and world were specifically made to conceal the guilt in our minds. The body was made so we would not know about guilt, yet it continually casts its shadows—the specialness we experience in the world. The problem is that we do not know its source. We know only that we live in a horrid world as bodies, to which awful things happen. We do not know all this is generated by thoughts in our minds, beneath the surface of our awareness.

Guilt continually spews forth its specialness and hate—of ourselves and others. Above all, it fuels the thought that says: "You have what you have taken from God; think not He has forgotten" (M-17.7:3-4). We then try to mitigate His punishment through pleading: "You do not have to punish me, Lord; You do not have to steal love back and destroy me. I will punish myself through a life of suffering; a life in which I atone for my sin." The magical hope is that if I punish myself, God will not have to. Despite my suffering, I will still be more merciful than God, whose "mercy" will be absolute. It must be so because I was absolutely merciless toward Him, and what I believe I did to Him I must believe He will do to me in return. And so in a magical attempt to diffuse the merciless fury of His vengeance, I inform Him that I will destroy this and that relationship. I will destroy my bank account. I will destroy this house and new car. Above all, I will destroy this body. I will eat foods I know I should not eat because they hurt me. That is how, unconsciously, I atone for my sin. My pain comes from my guilt, which comes from my need to be special.

If we never look at that specialness, there is no way we can ever undo it. What enabled us to get away with murder at the beginning was to ignore the Holy Spirit. If we had listened to His Voice, we would have abandoned the mad idea of special love. This becomes extremely important in terms of our personal lives; and it becomes even more important when we try to live and practice this Course. Even though we initially denied the Holy Spirit, if we were to listen to Him now we would give up the mad ideas of thievery, sacrifice, and *one or the other*; we would give up the insane idea of specialness as something we want; and we would return home. At that point our specialness, individuality, and autonomy would disappear, and all that would remain would be the Love of God.

We are taught in *A Course in Miracles* that linear time is an illusion. What seemed to have happened long ago is happening now because there is no time; only an illusion of time. When we projected the thought system of sin, guilt, and fear, the projection became past, present, and future. Linear time means we sinned in the past, feel guilty in the present, and fear the punishment that will come in the future. The ego thought system is thus the thought system of time. It is also the thought system of space, the projection of separation that began with the belief that there was a space or distance between us and God. In the physical universe we made up bodies that are separate from one another. Indeed, as physicists tell us, no two bodies can occupy the same place at the same time. Near the end of the text Jesus refers to this as the "gap" that keeps us separate from each other (e.g., T-28, 29). The thought of separation thus gave rise to a world of space; thoughts of sin, guilt, and fear to a world of time. They are the same:

> For time and space are one illusion, which takes different forms. If it has been projected beyond your mind you think of it as time. The nearer it is brought to where it is, the more you think of it in terms of space (T-26.VIII.1:3-5).

The "one illusion" is separation. What we believe we did in the original instant when we attacked God, we are still doing. This belief, which satisfies the continued existence of the ego and its specialness, is protected by our silencing the Holy Spirit's Voice.

That explains our resistance to *A Course in Miracles*—why we do not practice it, and why we read and forget these words almost as quickly as our eyes have rested on them. We have been programmed not to listen to the Holy Spirit's Voice of love, truth, and the Atonement, but to the voice of special love. "Yes," the ego says, "You should pay attention to God—but *my* God, who believes in specialness and loss, sacrifice and pain, bargaining and punishment, and who believes in *you* as a separate, special, and individual self." The instant we heard the ego's voice all formal religions were born, because they pay attention to a God who pays attention to us; the ego's answer to the true God Who did not notice us at all. But the God of specialness most certainly does pay attention! That is why people have so much trouble with this Course. The God of *A Course in Miracles* knows nothing of us, unless we distort the Course's teachings, and then make the Course's God like everyone else's God, and Jesus like everyone else's Jesus—believing in specialness, individuality, suffering and sacrifice, and the reality of the world.

Once again, all this—time, space, bodies, the allure of specialness, formal religions—is designed to prevent us from hearing the Holy Spirit's Voice. Most critical in keeping us from true hearing is *guilt*, which blinds us to the truth about the illusory world and its illusory source in our minds. Guilt blinds us—if I can mix perceptual metaphors—to hearing the Voice of the Holy Spirit, just as it blinds us as we read the words in this Course. As I said at the beginning, we do not want to look at our specialness, even though that is the core of *A Course in Miracles*. Even when he does not specifically use the word *specialness*, that is Jesus' reference in exhorting us to look at the ego, our special hate and special love relationships. Over and over he says to us: *Look, look, look!* But that, of course, is what the ego never wants us to do.

The ego knows that if we look at its thought system of specialness, we will let it go. Not only is it murderous and hurtful, it is insane. It does not give us what we want; indeed, it does us the exact opposite. It *takes* from us what we really want. We say we want happiness, love, and peace, but we do not know where to look for them. We seek in someone or something outside ourselves, but even when we think we have found what we are seeking, the voice of guilt says: "Yes, but you won't hold onto it. It will be taken from you." In the end that promise is fulfilled, of course, because our most special love of all will be lost—our very life. Thus do people love the made-up stories about afterlives. These mythologies become a way of cheating God, and we are always trying to cheat and steal from Him. But the guilt is overwhelming. Take the most extreme word or concept you can think of to describe the enormity of that guilt, and it still pales to insignificance in the face of its real nature. Guilt tells us we accomplished the impossible: we stole God's Life and Love; and guilt will see to it that we will never, ever change our minds. It sees to it again and again that our lives will be painful and miserable, and will be our just deserts: we deserve what we have coming to us.

This, then, is the ego's terrible thought system of specialness.

Chapter 2

OTHELLO: THE PLAY AND THE CHARACTERS

We will set aside the subject of specialness for a while to talk about the play itself, which will eventually bring us back to specialness. I will summarize the plot relatively quickly and then discuss its three main characters, focusing specifically on how they exemplify everything we have discussed so far. I will use two questions as the context for my discussion: What motivates Iago? and Why does Othello listen to him?

Othello is the second of Shakespeare's great tragedies. *Hamlet* came before, and *King Lear* and *Macbeth* followed. Of these four, *Othello* has probably upset its audience and readers the most. We are not going to spend time exploring the many reasons for this, except for the idea that Othello, unlike Shakespeare's other tragic heroes, seems so real and personal to us. His downfall is therefore particularly upsetting because it is the triumph of evil over good, the ego over God. Everyone, at least unconsciously, resonates to his defeat, given the fact that our greatest fear is that the ego is right and more powerful than God. Thus, despite *Othello*'s being a magnificent play and poetic masterpiece, our identification with the misguided Moor can yet arouse great antipathy in us.

The story centers on three main characters: Othello, his wife Desdemona, and Iago. Othello, the hero, is a general in the Venetian army, and Iago is his ensign. As we will see, Iago is probably the most outstanding example in all of literature of a purely evil individual and, as such, a perfect embodiment of the ego's thought system. Desdemona is one of several examples in Shakespeare of someone who is all good: virtuous, loving, kind, thoughtful, devoted, intelligent, and possessing a certain strength of character. She is the one who is betrayed and murdered. Othello, the play's protagonist, is the one who makes the wrong choice.

It is of note that although a general in the Venetian army, Othello is not Venetian or even Italian. He is a Moor. In fact, in the Italian tale from which Shakespeare drew his inspiration, he is not named, but simply referred to as "the Moor." Moors are a cross between Arabs and Berbers, the latter being a race from North Africa. The name *Moor* actually comes from *Mauri*, as does the name of North African country of Mauritania. Moors were dark skinned—though not black or Negro. In Shakespeare's play, however, Othello is black, and is portrayed and referred to that way throughout; one reason being that he is seen as an outsider. Yet he is an outsider who becomes a general in the army, loved and admired by almost everyone. Moreover, he marries the beautiful Desdemona, daughter of a wealthy and influential senator.

The courtship of Othello and Desdemona is the backdrop for the opening scene of the play. Because he was so highly respected, Othello was often invited to the house of Brabantio, Desdemona's father, where he and Desdemona became acquainted. He would regale her and her father with tales of his past glory and bravery. Desdemona fell in love with him, as did he with her. But the romance had to be carried on in secret, *sotto voce*, without Brabantio's knowledge, because the senator did not approve of his daughter marrying a man not of the same race or skin color. Thus the lovers used a go-between to exchange letters and other communications, a soldier by the name of Cassio. Eventually, Othello and Desdemona elope, and when Brabantio discovers it he goes before the senate to complain. He demands that something be done to Othello, who he is convinced abducted his daughter by seducing her through magic, since he is an alien. Othello defends himself in a simple and moving way; he obviously possesses a poetic soul. Of Shakespeare's great tragic heroes, Othello is probably the most soulful. Thus he speaks of his wooing of Desdemona:

> *She loved me for the dangers I had past;*
> *And I loved her that she did pity them.*

(I,iii,167)

The senators are convinced that magic was not the cause of elopement, but love—sincere and consensual. Desdemona speaks next, echoing the love of her spouse. The Duke, Venice's chief authority, accepts their explanation, and moves quickly to what he clearly sees as a far more important matter: the Turks' imminent invasion of Cyprus. He appoints Othello as the leader of the Venetian forces to withstand the attack. At roughly the same time, Othello appoints Cassio as his lieutenant, his number-two man. In doing so he overlooks Iago, even though his ensign is older and more experienced. Iago uses this situation as the ostensible reason for launching a plot against the general, and the rest of the play deals with Iago's plot of vengeance—to destroy

Othello for having chosen Cassio over him. As we will see, this really is not Iago's primary reason, but an excuse to act out a much deeper motivation. Iago sees that Desdemona is the dearest thing in the world to Othello, and therefore he focuses his plot on convincing the Moor that Desdemona has been unfaithful, and, indeed, has been having a clandestine affair with Cassio. I will not go into Iago's specific machinations; suffice it to say, he succeeds in bringing about Othello's downfall.

Despite one's abhorrence of Iago, who is truly as evil as a person can get, one must still stand in awe of his skill in successfully accomplishing his goal. He is an artist at work, brilliant in his artistry. He does not have a step-by-step strategy, but simply takes events as they come, weaving them into a web in which he ultimately ensnares the unknowing Othello. Circumstances work to his advantage, and Othello follows Iago as an ass is led by the nose, as we shall see presently.

When Othello finally becomes convinced of Desdemona's infidelity, entirely an invention of Iago, he decides she must be killed. Although he seems to hesitate before the murder—he is still very much in love with her—he remains steadfast as he strangles her. Kissing her three times, he kills her. Only when the deed is done does the truth emerge, and Othello realizes he was duped by Iago, who had made up stories and planted false evidence. He tries to kill his "friend," but only succeeds in wounding him. Iago is apprehended, and is about the only one of Shakespeare's villains who does not get killed. At the end, the instructions are that he is to be tortured, with the implication that he will be killed, but that does not happen before the play ends. Finally, Othello takes out a hidden dagger and kills himself.

There are, again, two major questions confronting the reader of this play. The obvious reason for the first—*What really motivates Iago to exact vengeance on Othello?*—is that Othello appointed Cassio rather than himself, yet this is not very convincing. For example, Iago soon works it out so that Cassio, who cannot hold his liquor, gets drunk. A quite displeased Othello demotes him, and then appoints Iago as his lieutenant instead. Iago thus got what he ostensibly wanted. The explanation that Iago was avenging himself on Othello for choosing Cassio is not compelling.

The second question—*Why does Othello trust Iago?*—relates to why people find this play so upsetting. He is not a stupid man. Why does he not question Desdemona? He confronts her, but never gives her a chance to set the record straight. Instead, he believes Iago's lies, and once convinced of Desdemona's unfaithfulness, kills her without even a moment's hesitation. Why, even though he loves her more than anything, right up to the moment of her death, and afterwards?

Freud, as already observed in my introduction in Volume I, was a great lover of Shakespeare, and in his observations on *Hamlet* stated his belief that psychoanalysis was able to solve the 300-year-old problem of why Hamlet hesitated—why he failed to act immediately to avenge his father's murder. Hamlet was a man of courage, as he demonstrates at other times in the play, but he could not bring himself to kill his uncle, his father's murderer, until the play's very end. Freud's answer was that Hamlet's Oedipus complex, with its conflict and guilt, stopped him from taking the obvious, rather straightforward action.

Just as Freud found an answer to the puzzle of Hamlet's motivations and conflict, *A Course in Miracles* provides an answer to our two questions about Iago and Othello, to which we now turn.

What Motivates Iago?

As I have said, Iago is the epitome of evil; a man basically devoid of feeling. Cold and passionless, he boasts that he is master of his emotions, saying at one point:

> *Ere* [before] *I would say, I would drown myself for the love of a guinea hen* [fall in love with a woman]*, I would change my humanity with a baboon.*

(I,iii,315)

In other words, he would never allow himself to be overwhelmed with passion. His marriage to Emilia is clearly a loveless one, and she eventually is the source of his downfall. Being above feelings, Iago says of love:

> *It is merely a lust of the blood and a permission of the will.*

(I,iii,337)

However, Iago's most outstanding trait, and one that links him directly to the ego, is that he does not appear to be what he is. He says it himself:

> *I am not what I am.*

(I,i,65)

At least fifteen times in the play he is referred to as honest. Most of those references come from Othello, but he is also described that way by others. In fact there are times when Iago ironically uses the term *honesty* to describe himself. He comes across as so sincere, honest, faithful, and true that no one, not even his wife, knows what he is really about. And that is what the ego is like as well. It seems to be truthful; and its perceptions of truth are what we accept as truth. We never question them. When Iago's wife Emilia sees Othello becoming crazed with jealousy and anger, she expresses how someone must have done this to him, because this is not the Othello she knows. It never occurs to her that the "someone" is her husband. That is Iago's craftiness: no one suspected. Even the people he included in his plotting thought he was honest and only had everyone's interests at heart.

What allows Iago to get away with this deception is the confusion of *form* and *content*, familiar to all students of *A Course in Miracles*. Iago mocks everyone because they pay attention to his form. Later we will see Iago's citation of the devil's evil work (the *content*) first masquerading as Heaven (the *form*). Iago's circle looked to the form, but Iago alone was aware of the content. Thus he laughed at everyone who was taken in by his honesty, which so successfully disguised his inherent dishonesty.

Before discussing Iago's true motivation, let me point out one other reason that Iago himself gives—twice—for his vengeance: people talking about an affair Othello had with Emilia. This would certainly justify Iago's desire for revenge. However, there is no basis in the play for this at all; nothing in the contacts between Othello and Emilia that substantiate that story, and it is not referred to by any other character. In other words, this story, in addition to Cassio's appointment as lieutenant, are really Iago's ways of justifying to himself his malicious actions against Othello.

Why, then, does Iago act as he does? To state it very simply, he hates what is good. Above all, he hates that Othello has *chosen* goodness. Othello *chose* to marry Desdemona, a virtuous woman, about whom no one says anything negative, speaking of her only with the highest regard. Even Othello, as he is about to kill her, praises her highly, setting aside for an instant his convictions of infidelity. Likewise, Iago does not really hate Cassio, a good man who was appointed in his place. He hates that Othello *chose* Cassio. We see in Iago a manifestation of, if not equation with the ego. As I explained earlier, the ego does not hate God, Whom it does not know. Similarly, it does not hate love nor seek to destroy it. It hates the power of the Son's mind to *choose* for love and against the ego. That is what Iago holds against Othello—*his ability to choose love and what is good.*

We have already seen that in the early parts of the play Othello is presented as having everything a man could want. I will return to this theme later, but this is clearly Iago's view. He even has fortune on his side, because when he sets sail to defend Cyprus against the invading Turks, a huge storm comes up and sinks the Turkish fleet. The general is victorious without even having to fight. Everything goes Othello's way and Iago cannot stand it, especially since he has chosen against Iago. Thus Iago's motivation: to destroy the one person in the world who has power over him. He seeks vengeance against Othello, not because of Cassio, not because he suspects Othello of having an affair with Emilia, but because Othello chose against him—in the ultimate sense of that word. And so he seeks to bring about his downfall.

Twice in the play Iago says, "*I hate the Moor.*" He says it once to his henchman, Roderigo, so that can be seen as calculating (I,iii,370); but then he says it when he is alone (I,iii,389). He also says some other things about Othello, which in a sense are expressions of admiration for Othello's goodness, only to be followed by expressions of disrespect for him. For instance:

> [Othello] *holds me well;*
> *The better shall my purpose work on him.*

> (I,iii,392)

In other words, Othello trusts me; therefore, he believes anything I say to him. This is the same as our relationship with the ego: anything the ego says to us we accept as true because we have excluded the Voice of love. Othello deems Iago to be honest, and therefore accepts anything he says as the truth:

> *The Moor is of a free and open nature,*
> *That thinks men honest that but seem to be so;*

Thus, Othello thinks that Iago is honest, but he only seems to be honest.

> *And will as tenderly be led by th' nose*
> *As asses are.*

And that is exactly what he does.

Iago then continues:

I have't;–it is engender'd [I have the plan; the plan now is caused]:–
hell and night
Must bring this monstrous birth to the world's light.

(I,iii,401)

A little later he says:

The Moor–howbeit that I endure him not–
Is of a constant, loving, noble nature...

(II,i,292)

So there is nothing bad about Othello, except that he is good. And still later:

Make the Moor thank me, love me, and reward me,
For making him egregiously an ass,
And practising upon his peace and quiet
Even to madness. 'Tis here, but yet confused:
Knavery's plain face is never seen till used.

(II,i,312)

Iago knows his audience, and so he exclaims:

Divinity of hell!
When devils will their blackest sins put on,
They do suggest at first with heavenly shows,
As I do now...

(II,iii,349)

When devils want to do their dirtiest, blackest, most evil work, they first cloak it in holy garb—*"heavenly shows"*—so that it seems to be something it is not. The Bible, for example, which from the perspective of *A Course in Miracles* is written largely by the ego, seems to be so holy, spiritual, and religious—all about God, Love, Heaven, and so forth. Only when you read it carefully do you recognize the thought system of specialness that underlies it. That is what Iago means: *When devils will their blackest sins put on, They do suggest at first with heavenly shows, As I do now.*

As we have seen, everyone thinks Iago to be honest. There is the scene, for example, when a maddened Othello rants and raves at Iago, who, craftily putting on the "face of innocence," replies that this is what he gets for being honest. Othello quickly recants, saying in effect: "I am so sorry I did not trust you; you are the one person I can trust."

Finally Iago says of Desdemona:

So will I turn her virtue into pitch [pitch is black];
And out of her own goodness make the net
That shall enmesh them all.

(II,iii,359)

And in the next act, as he sees Othello begin to be infected with his lies, he says:

The Moor already changes with my poison…

(III,iii,325)

Iago plots so that people will not suspect him of knavery—of what he is really doing—until it is already done. That is what the ego has done with us. Having silenced the Holy Spirit's Voice, all we listen to is the ego. It tricks us by making up stories that we then believe. Likewise, Iago cleverly made up a totally untrue story about Desdemona's infidelity, and came up with false witnesses to corroborate it, giving specific expression to the ego's ontological plan. It made up a fantastic story about our infidelity to God and His to us, wherein He betrays His Love for His Son by seeking to murder him. We not only bought the ego's lies without questioning them at all, we still do. We actually think—despite what our intellect tells us as students of *A Course in Miracles*—we live here in a body. That is the greatest lie of all, but how can we deny it? We think our senses are honest witnesses. Thus— my body feels sensation, looks in the mirror and sees something, responds to your body; your body thinks mine is here, and my body thinks yours is here. Whether we love or hate each other, we certainly believe we are here. And that is because we are creatures of perception, and perception lies.

Form is always what we perceive. Recall this statement from the text: "Nothing so blinding as perception of form" (T-22.III.6:7). Perception lies. Seeing only form, our eyes literally lie, for in truth there is no world out there. We perceive an illusory world of separation that is a projection of an illusory thought of separation. A lie has begotten a lie. Yet the body, an intrinsic part of the lie, tells us it is the truth. Returning to *Othello*, our hero "saw" and "heard" what Iago wanted him to see and hear. Adding up what he thought was two and two, he got the wrong number. As we all do. That, again, is why this is such a powerful play: it speaks to all of us.

There is no hope as long as we listen to the wrong voice. As we will see, Othello is aware that there is no hope, for he has turned away from his true hope—the voice of truth. This course helps us learn how to listen to that voice. Our learning first entails being aware we are listening to the wrong voice, identifying it as the ego. Only then can we begin to understand the difference between the ego's honesty and the Holy Spirit's. What goes for honesty in this world is a lie, for it is expressed and experienced by a body, the most dishonest witness of all.

We have therefore all listened to the ego's voice, and it has egregiously led us like an ass to slaughter, because in the end we die. This happens because we never question the ego, or suspect there might be something wrong with what it tells us. When Iago begins his deceitful work, Othello protests, saying that Desdemona would never be unfaithful. But as Iago presents him with one lie after another, one piece of circumstantial evidence after another, Othello quickly allows himself to succumb to the deception.

Again, we have all been duped like Othello. Even if we at times question what goes on in our world, we do not question the fundamental assumption that underlies everything we experience. We read this Course that comes to us from the Voice of truth and Love, and we agree; we yes it to death! And then we alter it so that it ends up supporting the lie of our individual existence; that our bodies are real and can know reality, and that God is a separate Person. We do not question the ego's voice because it seems to be so honest. We do not question the body because our bodies seem such reliable witnesses. It is only when we see the outcomes that we finally throw up our hands and say: "Oh, my God, what have I have done!" That is the point Jesus describes near the beginning of the text where he says:

> Tolerance for pain may be high, but it is not without limit. Eventually everyone begins to recognize, however dimly, that there *must* be a better way. As this recognition becomes more firmly established, it becomes a turningpoint (T-2.III.3:5-7).

It is only when our pain becomes intolerable that we begin to question, the point the ego and the world's Iagos desperately try to prevent.

Verdi's *Otello*: Iago's Credo

We have included in the Appendix a speech by Iago called Iago's Credo, and you will notice that Shakespeare's name does not appear as the author. That is because he did not write it. It is instead from Verdi's opera *Otello*, the libretto having been written by a rather well-regarded Italian poet of the 19th century, Arrigo Boito. Let me say a few words about the opera as a way of introducing this speech.

Otello (Italian for *Othello*) was the second to the last of Verdi's operas. He wrote it when he was in his early seventies, which was quite an achievement. About fifteen years had passed since his previous masterpiece, *Aida*, and he had stopped composing operas. He had always been enamored of Shakespeare, whom he respected greatly, and earlier in his life had composed a relatively unremarkable *Macbeth*. In response to repeated suggestions and urgings, he finally agreed to compose *Otello* with Boito, an operatic composer as well as an accomplished poet. He is best known for *Mephistopheles*, based on the Faust legend, and part of the standard repertory. Moreover, this musician and poet loved Shakespeare as much as Verdi—a suitable partner for the great composer.

Any opera lover who has been embarrassed by one dreadful libretto after another is very grateful for *Otello*. It is that rare Italian opera whose libretto needs no apology and is commensurate with the composer's genius. The operatic story and libretto are brilliant because they are completely faithful to Shakespeare. I would not be so heretical to suggest that it is better than Shakespeare's play but, as drama, it comes pretty close. Boito used Shakespeare's major scenes and often quoted the play word for word. Moreover, he understood each character extremely well as, needless to say, did Verdi, who masterfully depicted them in his music. From start to finish it is a brilliant opera—musically and dramatically—and those making its acquaintance for the first time have a real treat in store for them.

There are many places in the play where Iago expresses his beliefs, and we have already read some of them. Boito synthesized, not the words, but the *content* of Iago's beliefs, and fashioned them into his Credo, which means "I believe" in Latin and Italian. In Shakespeare, Iago never actually states that he believes in a cruel God, as is stated at the beginning of this aria. But, as we have seen, he embodies and reflects the very thought system that must include the belief that God is cruel. That is why I put the parallel passage from the text next to it in the Appendix; it is not exactly parallel in words, but certainly in content. We will now go through Iago's Credo, this powerful depiction of the ego's thought system:

I believe in a cruel God, who has created me
In his image and whom, in anger, I name.

To summarize our earlier account of the origin and nature of specialness: We are the ones who "created" God in our own cruel image;
cruel because our self was made by selfishly and cruelly destroying
God. How much more cruel can you get than to murder love? All God
did was love us, and we decided His Love was not enough and not
what we wanted. Thus we did Him one better and sacrificed Him—the
height of selfish cruelty!—projecting that self-image to make up a God
Who is cruel. It is not only in the Bible that we see this image; we find
it in many other places as well. For instance, one of the faces of God
in Hinduism is Kali, the destroyer God. Returning to the Western God,
He is clearly a destroyer along with being a creator: a deity who loves,
forgives, and is merciful; yet a deity who also gets angry, is jealous,
and destroys—in other words, a god we have made in the image and
likeness of our specialness.

From some vile germ or atom
Am I born.
I am wicked
Because I am human;
And I feel the primeval slime in me.

This is quite similar to what *A Course in Miracles* describes as the
belief that we "are the home of evil, darkness and sin" (W-pI.93.1:1),
which is what each of us, deep within, believes about ourselves. The
very fact we are born means we have come from some *"vile germ,"* the
ego thought system that says we exist at God's expense; in order to
have our selfish needs met, God had to be destroyed. It is from that
"germ," that cruel thought, that we all are fashioned. It is *"primeval"*
in the sense that it is ontological, and *"slime"* because of sin and guilt.
As I frequently say, nice people do not come into this world; they stay
at home with God. It is the slimy ones, the vile germs of guilt who
come here.

Yes! This is my creed!
I believe with a firm heart, as ever does
The widow praying at the temple,
That whatever evil I think or do
Was decreed for me by fate.

That is what life is like. As we will see in the next stanza, Iago says he does not believe anyone is really good; and that idea is without a doubt in the spirit of Shakespeare's Iago, who did not believe anyone was good, either—my *"evil... was decreed for me by fate."* It clearly also reflected Shakespeare's observations of human beings. From *A Course in Miracles* we understand, too, that no one here is good. We are here because our guilt told us we are evil. A personal and direct way of relating to this is by understanding evil as selfishness, something with which we can all identify. We do not care about others, except to the extent to which they meet our needs. We care only about ourselves: preserving our lives, identity, and specialness. We use everyone and everything to further that aim. Similarly, in the play Iago uses those around him to further his aim of destroying Othello: Emilia, Cassio, Desdemona, and Roderigo. He used everyone as fabric in his web to achieve his own cruel and selfish goal.

> *I believe that a just man is but an hysterical actor,*
> *Both in face and heart,*
> *That everything in him is a lie:*
> *Tears, kisses, glances,*
> *Sacrifices and honor.*

Everything here *is* a lie, because, to cite the Bard: *"All the world's a stage"* (*As You Like It*, II,vii,139). Boito here uses the Shakespearean image of the actor to emphasize Iago's credo that we all play a part, and this role playing constitutes the lie. *A Course in Miracles* helps us understand this. The section entitled "Dream Roles" (T-29.IV) explains that we are all dreaming, and we cast everyone in roles so they will meet our needs. Whenever we get angry, it is because people have not fulfilled the roles we assigned them in our dreams. They have not met our needs the way we demanded they be met, and therefore deserve our wrath and vengeance. They deserve to be killed, and we are justified in killing them off in one way or another.

Thus this world is a setup, a stage on which we act out the play we wrote. We are the authors, stars, casting and acting directors, producers, and so on. We dictate what every character in our dramas will do and say. Thus everyone plays the role I have assigned them in my play, just as I play a role in everyone else's play. We all do the same thing; so no one should be taken at face value. Iago knows that better than anyone, because all give him the face value of honesty, as I mentioned earlier;

and only he knows the truth. When you extrapolate from that to our own lives, the problem is that we think we are about something other than what we actually are, which is fulfilling our specialness—the purpose of our being here. We then seek to blame everyone else for not having what we want. We think we are about being successful, helpful, loving, and kind; about being good parents, children, and friends—good this and good that. But it is all nothing more than a means of acting out the ego's plot and fulfilling its clever strategy.

> *And I believe man to be fortune's fool* [borrowed from *Romeo and*
> *Juliet*]
> *From the germ of the cradle*
> *To the worm of the grave.*

Those of you who know *Hamlet* may remember that our melancholy Dane talks about worms devouring worms (IV,iii,20). In fact, there is a passage in the manual that draws upon this very speech (M-27.3).[5] Iago has already told us that the *"germ of the cradle"* is *"vile germ"* and *"primeval slime."* He tells us here we will all end up in the grave, eaten by worms. In other words, life means absolutely nothing:

> *And after all this mockery....*

This is no different from what Jesus tells us in *A Course in Miracles*, but it is stated from Iago's wrong-minded point of view. What we call life—everything here—is a mockery, travesty, and parody of life. There is no life here at all, as we see in the following passage from *A Course in Miracles*:

> Where God created life, there life must be. In any state apart from Heaven life is illusion. At best it seems like life; at worst, like death. Yet both are judgments on what is not life, equal in their inaccuracy and lack of meaning (T-23.II.19:2-5).

Iago again:

> *And after all this mockery comes Death.*
> *And then? And then? Death is nothingness,*
> *And Heaven is an ancient lie.*

The ego tells us there is nothing here but meaninglessness—the meaningless of life punctuated by the meaninglessness of death, after

---

5. See my discussion in Volume II: *Hamlet*, pp. 47-52.

which is nothingness. Yet we cover over this belief in oblivion, as Iago has covered over his wickedness, so that it seems to be something else—the special selves hell-bent on finding the special objects to fulfill their special needs.

Alongside Iago's Credo in the Appendix is the aforementioned passage from the text in which Jesus describes the true nature of this world: a place of suffering, pain, and loss, until finally:

> …bodies wither and gasp and are laid in the ground, and are no more (T-13.in.2:10).

That is the same perspective we find expressed in Iago's Credo. And then the last line:

> Not one of them but has thought that God is cruel (2:11).

Thus, again, Iago begins his Credo with a statement about his "cruel God," and Jesus ends with a similar statement. Once we believe we exist as bodies, we must believe God is cruel. We must, because we got here by being cruel to God. Inevitably, its unbearable pain caused us to project the guilt over our cruelty, which is intrinsic to our very existence. The projection of our guilt reflects the law of mind—what is within must be projected out, *unless* we look at it. If we look honestly upon the guilt and its foundation, it disappears. But obviously, guilt tells us *not* to look, and so we project it out, thinking we are not the ones who are cruel, God is!

When the ego begins to weave its web of specialness, it makes up a story of God's cruelty: Yes, we attacked God first, but He is coming back. The fear that story engenders becomes our motivation for leaving the mind and making up a world, magically hoping that we can leave everything behind us. The fact of the matter is, however, that we bring everything with us: *ideas leave not their source.* We have never left the mind, just as when sleeping at night we have the illusion of being wherever the dream is taking us. We remain asleep, and everything in the dream happens in our minds; not in some other country, not with other people. Only in our minds.

It is the same situation with our lives here in the world. We are asleep and dreaming—"at home in God, dreaming of exile" (T-10.I.2:1)—and think the dream is real because the "honest" voice of the ego tells us it is so. The witnesses of the body that tell us the world is real have to be believed, just as Othello had to believe the circumstantial evidence that

Iago presented. At one point, for example, Iago has Cassio talking about his mistress, Bianca, and Othello thinks he is talking about Desdemona. So Othello again adds up the wrong numbers and reaches the wrong conclusion. Iago's wife Emilia is Desdemona's friend, becoming both her servant and confidant. And so Iago has her steal a handkerchief that Othello had given his wife, a handkerchief that had tremendous meaning for Othello. After obtaining the handkerchief, Iago plants it on Cassio, where it can be seen by the jealous Moor. Once again, Othello believes his lying perception, thinking that Desdemona gave the handkerchief to Cassio.

That is what we all do. Deceived by the ego's lies, we trust our eyes and ears to tell us what is true. We do it on the gross physical level, actually thinking there is a world out there, and that people are there to interact with. Without ever questioning it, we believe that to be the truth. We are deceived on a more subtle level as well, believing our *interpretations* of what we perceive to be happening out there. We are sure we understand why people do what they do; we are sure that we know what they think, and why they are thinking it. Someone may be having a bad day, and we immediately personalize it, concluding that the person does not like us. The upset, in fact, had nothing to do with us, but our guilt says we deserve to be punished. As is described in "The Obstacles to Peace," we send out hungry dogs of fear that look for guilt in others, pounce on it, and bring it back to be devoured (T-19.IV-A.i). We want to find fault with people. We want to find things in the world that will prove how terrible others are, or how terrible we are. We actually believe what these witnesses of guilt bring back to us, just as Othello believed what Iago told him and "demonstrated" was true.

Othello saw with his eyes, heard with his ears, and interpreted with his brain, as all do—and he was wrong. Even though we have not yet discussed Othello in any depth, we can begin to see why people find this play to be so disturbing. Like the Moor, we are taken in by the ego's malevolent voice that sounds so honest and caring—and yet deceives us about everything it is doing. That is the source of the play's terrifying nature—the painful consequences of being deceived. Here is a man who had everything and ends up with nothing. Othello is married to this wonderful and faithful woman whom he loves and trusts; *and he does not listen to her.* We have within us the Voice of love, the presence of Jesus in our minds and in this Course; and we still do not

listen to him. We judge, hate, criticize, and find fault; we worship at
the shrine of our specialness. This play upsets us so because we fear
we will end up like poor Othello—destroyed by the ego, having denied
the power of love.

We turn now to Shakespeare's hero and the second big question:
Why would he ever listen to Iago?

Why Did Othello Listen to Iago?

Let me briefly review the status of things, just before Iago began his
devious work. Othello had the world at his fingertips: He had the
woman of his dreams, who adored him as he adored her. He had the
respect of everyone in Venice. He was the successful general in command of the army, winning one battle after another. He even had the
gods on his side, because a storm destroyed the Turks and he lost not
a single person or ship in the victory.

Now our question: Given his love for Desdemona, why would he
listen to Iago, even though he had trusted him in the past? The answer
is found in the teachings of *A Course in Miracles*. Othello had everything, yet his ego whispered to him that he stole it. In one sense he did
steal Desdemona, because they were married behind her father's back.
Brabantio did not know they were courting, nor that when Cassio vis-
ited, he was serving as a courier between the lovers. The courtship and
marriage were thus carried out secretly—stolen love as it were. Within
the ego thought system success is interpreted as theft: *you have what
you have taken* (T-23.II.9:2-3).

It is interesting that after Othello speaks to the senate, convincing
everyone he did nothing wrong and had not seduced Desdemona with
magic—his wooing consisted solely in speaking of his heroic life—
Brabantio, in conceding defeat, says to Othello (quite prophetically in
light of what happens later):

> Look to her, Moor, if thou hast eyes to see:
> She has deceived her father, and may thee.

(I,iii,293)

That did not turn out to be true in terms of anything Desdemona did,
but it was certainly true in terms of Othello's guilt. Guilt demands punishment, and so Othello would have thought unconsciously that having

stolen love, he deserved to have it stolen from him. Brabantio's words fired his guilt, the flames of which he himself fanned. Interestingly, later in the play, Iago, who was not aware of what Brabantio said, says the very same thing to Othello:

> *She did deceive her father, marrying you;*
> *And when she seem'd to shake and fear your looks,*
> *She loved them most.*

(III,iii,206)

Iago is asking Othello why he would think she is not capable of deceiving him, when she has already deceived her father. All women are like that, Iago adds. The reason Othello would be taken in was that his guilt demanded punishment. The reason his eyes and ears would believe what Iago said, and the phony evidence he planted, was that he secretly *wanted* to believe it. The only way he could atone for his sin of stealing Desdemona's love (a metaphor for stealing love from God) was to punish himself, thereby forestalling God's punishment of him. Thus he did what everyone does: unconsciously sabotaging himself so that God would not punish him.

Bodies were made to sabotage us. Since our lives are nothing but a dream we ourselves spun, we could have made our bodies in any number of ways. Why did we make them to be such absolute failures—a source of pain and suffering—for ourselves and everyone else? Because that is how we mitigate the punishment we expect from God, telling Him in effect: "Yes, I sinned against you, and am very sorry for it. But you do not have to punish me; I will take care of it myself." For example, I get a new car and my ego says: "If you have it, you must have stolen it." I drive the car, and before long I have an accident. Everyone is aware of that dynamic, because we all have lived it out one way or another—sometimes in dramatic fashion such as having an accident with a brand new car; other times more subtly. Likewise, we will sabotage relationships unconsciously. Secretly, we *want* people to betray us, to be unfaithful and walk out on us, for our egos tell us that is what we have coming to us. That is why on some level Othello— even though this is not suggested in the play—would have known he should not be trusting Iago. Initially, his instinct is to defend Desdemona when Iago begins to weave his web, but as Iago provides one piece of evidence after another, one lie after another, Othello succumbs to the deception.

It is interesting that Othello never asks Desdemona about Iago's stories; nor Cassio or Emilia, Desdemona's closest friend and confidante—one reason the audience becomes furious with him. When Othello confronts Desdemona and asks about the handkerchief he already believes she has given to Cassio, he is not seeking the truth but simply attempting to trap her. He does not ask the voice of love to tell him the truth, because his guilt demands that he listen only to its voice and accept the punishment that he believes is forthcoming. Incidentally, we see this same dynamic at work in our relationship with Jesus. So often when we go to him for help we have already made up our minds. We ask his help with what we already set him up to help with—some specific problem—so that he will fail us. When it does not turn out the way we want, we feel justified in accusing him, just as we have accused God, of not giving us the specialness that we want.

Returning to Othello, by condemning Desdemona without asking her to explain the charges of infidelity, he takes a perfectly noble, good, and happy life and destroys it out of his own guilt, no different from what we all do. If things work out well, there is the ego's little voice that says: "What you have, you stole. You have what you have taken; therefore, it will be taken back." This is the now-familiar fourth law of chaos: Your brother has taken innocent love and hidden it where you would never think to look: in his body. In order to get it, you must take it from there, which means that ultimately you will have to kill in order to get the love you want (T-23.II.9-11).

Thus Othello's secret motivation is to pay himself back for his sin, and so he undermines his successful life. As I mentioned above, he attempts to argue with Iago as he begins to make up his story:

If she be false, O, then heaven mocks itself!

(III,iii,278)

He cannot believe Desdemona would be false. Even before Iago started weaving his tale, Othello was musing on his love for Desdemona:

Perdition catch my soul,
But I do love thee! and when I love thee not,
Chaos is come again.

(III,iii,90)

That wonderfully expresses the nature of special love: "*When I love thee not, chaos is come again.*" In one sense this is a harbinger of later happenings in the play, because chaos does come when Othello "ceases" to love Desdemona, at least to the extent that his mistrust leads to her death at his hand. In the context of the dynamics of specialness, it is true that without special love we have only chaos, for it is the ego's device to protect us from the horror of our guilt: I need your love to prevent me from feeling the horror of my self-loathing; I need you to tell me I am whole to cover up the pain of my loneliness and isolation; I need your comfort to conceal the pain of believing I destroyed Heaven, leaving me bereft and alone; I need you to be a false god, an idol that will take the place of the true God. But when your love is absent; when your attention, devotion, and admiration are withheld, chaos is come again. That is why we are all so attracted to specialness. It keeps us firmly rooted in the body, whether we are talking about a special relationship with another person, an object, substance, thing, or idea—*A Course in Miracles* itself. The form does not matter. As long as I have that certain special something I no longer have to deal with my mind's pain.

In the play's final scene, Othello goes into Desdemona's bedchamber to kill her, and will not be dissuaded by anyone, including himself. There is a lamp burning as he enters, and he says this tragic *double entendre*:

> *Put out the light, and then,–put out the light:*

The first light he is putting out is the lamp, to darken the deed; and then the light of Desdemona's life. In musing on these two he says:

> *If I quench thee, thou flaming minister* [he is talking about the
>   lamp],
> *I can again thy former light restore,*
> *Should I repent me* [if I change my mind, I can always re-light the
>   lamp];–*but once put out thy light,*

And now he is looking at Desdemona, who is asleep:

> *Thou cunning'st pattern of excelling nature,*
> *I know not where is that Promethean heat*
> *That can thy light relume.*

In other words: there is no light in all the gods—Prometheus is the god, remember, who stole fire from Zeus—that can re-illuminate the light of your life, once he takes it.

When I have plucked the rose,
I cannot give it vital growth again,
It needs must wither:—I'll smell it on the tree.—

(V,ii,7)

He will smell life's rose on the tree, but when it is gone, so is its sweet fragrance. That is the tragedy, and the fear that possesses all of us: Once we choose the ego, our choice will be irrevocable. When we chose to put out the light of Heaven, it was out; unlike the artificial light of a candle, oil lamp, or electric light. When we extinguished the light of love by our desire for specialness, it was gone. That is the tragedy: Nothing in this world has the power to bring that light back.

To digress briefly and to amplify on a point made in my introduction to these volumes on Shakespeare's tragedies,[6] just as Macbeth knew the consequences of his decision to kill King Duncan and was overwhelmed with guilt, Othello, though not consciously guilty, knew the consequences of his actions. For this reason Macbeth's was more of a psychological tragedy, whereas Othello's is more external, at least on the surface. In that sense *Macbeth* is the more psychologically powerful play, because of its penetrating read of Macbeth's psyche as he struggles with his guilt, which ends up being acted out by his wife. Othello does not struggle in this way at all. He cannot stop himself even though he knows he is making an irrevocable choice, and does not attempt to— reminiscent of Freud's *repetition compulsion*, the neurotic inner drive that compels one to repeat behavior that inevitably results in pain. I am here focusing on the ontological level: the fear that in love's presence, we would destroy it. This, then, is the ultimate tragedy.

Othello is thus aware of the consequences of what he is about to do. He will put out Desdemona's light, and then it is finished, reminiscent of Iago's Credo.

Othello extinguishes the light, and then looks adoringly at his sleeping wife. He kisses her, saying:

O balmy breath, that dost almost persuade
Justice to break her sword!—

I am almost tempted to "break [my] sword," he says, but justice decrees she be killed because of what she has done. Yet she looks so beautiful and innocent....

---

6. See the beginning of Volume I, *King Lear – Love and Be Silent*.

One more, one more [meaning one more kiss. And he kisses her
 again],
Be thus when thou art dead, and I will kill thee,
And love thee after.–

Be like this—this innocent angel—and after you die, and I die, I will
be with you again. But this is something I must do.

One more [one more kiss]*, and this the last*
So sweet was ne'er so fatal. I must weep,
But they are cruel tears: this sorrow's heavenly;
It strikes where it doth love.

(V,ii,16)

He is going to kill the one thing—the only thing in the universe—he
truly loves, and it is as though he cannot help himself. Never once,
again, did he try to discover the truth, because he committed to the
voice of the lie.

Othello awakens Desdemona, who pleads with him not to kill her,
for she had had a premonition of her fate and, in fact, had Emilia bring
out her wedding dress that evening. Thus she, too, allowed her fate to
be sealed. She asks Othello to spare her, at least until morning, with
the empty expectation the situation could be resolved differently and
the truth be known. But he rejects her plea: No, it has to be done now.
He smothers her with a pillow and she lays dying. Everyone now
rushes in, Emilia first, who demands: *"O who hath done this deed?"*
Desdemona, faithful to her husband to the end, not so different in content from Cordelia, Lear's faithful daughter, answers: *"Nobody,—I*
myself." (V,ii,124). And then she dies, without a trace of retribution in
her heart or in her words. Iago now enters, and then Cassio. The truth
is finally revealed as Emilia divulges the true tale of the handkerchief.
Letters setting out the plot in Iago's handwriting are also found. At last
Othello realizes his wife's innocence, but there is nothing he can do.
The light has been put out.

Othello surrenders his sword, and makes a brief speech—the story
of one *"that loved not wisely, but too well."* In his final act he removes
a dagger, hidden on his person, and stabs himself; murmuring these
very moving lines:

I kissed thee, ere I killed thee:–no way but this,
Killing myself, to die upon a kiss.

(V,ii,359)

He falls over his wife, kisses her, and dies. Cassio is named governor of Cyprus, as the play ends.

It is a great tribute to Othello as a character that no matter how many times we read or see the play, or hear the opera, there remains the hope that somehow this time Othello will not do it. He ceases being a character in a play, but assumes the dimensions of a real person— ourselves. At the very end, especially when he looks at Desdemona with such love and kisses her, there is yet something in us that implores him: "This time, choose differently." And, of course, he does not.

Verdi gave a wonderful touch to the play's ending, beyond even the genius of the world's greatest dramatist, because he was working with music as well as words. The music in this deeply moving final scene recalls a moment from the end of Act One, Othello and Desdemona's love duet that closes with a beautiful theme of their love, highlighting their kiss. That kiss motif is heard again in the opera's close when Othello enters the bedchamber. It is an indication that Othello is thinking about their love at the very instant he is planning to extinguish it; caught between what he loves most and his ego's guilt. That poignant musical motif is then heard. Othello kisses Desdemona three times and suffocates her; and when he kills himself, he falls upon her saying: "*A kiss, another kiss, and one last kiss*" (in Italian: *un bacio, un bacio ancora, un altro bacio),* but he expires before uttering the last syllable, as the kiss motif is heard for the last time.

This is a tragedy. It is not a play of Atonement, repentance, or forgiveness. *Othello* reflects to us that all is indeed lost when we choose to follow the ego, for we will have inevitably killed the very thing we love, symbolized by Desdemona. She is a symbol of the Love of God we believe we have killed; and that we continue to kill. Our guilt demands that we be punished, and that is why this is such a compelling and upsetting play for almost everyone who reads it. It portrays what we secretly feel so guilty about: we did it once, we did it again, and we will continue to murder love so that our specialness will survive, despite its tremendous cost to us.

Chapter 3

A COURSE IN MIRACLES: OTHELLO AND THE EGO

We now look at some passages in *A Course in Miracles*, primarily in the text, that elaborate on what we have discussed. First, some passages pertaining to our earlier theme: asking God for special favor. We next turn to readings that deal with our need to drown out the Voice of the Holy Spirit with the voice of specialness. This is followed by passages that deal specifically with the dynamic of guilt demanding punishment, Othello's motivation to destroy his life. In the final chapter we examine passages in *A Course in Miracles* that give us the other side: the alternative Othello did not choose. Thus, the three sets of passages in this chapter explore the ego, while we close by looking at how one gets beyond the ego's specialness and guilt. I will not leave you lying in the blood-drenched sheets of special relationships.

Asking God for Special Favor

We begin with Chapter 13 in the text and the all-important section entitled "The Fear of Redemption." We find in this section a powerfully clear expression of our fear of God's Love. Paragraphs 10 and 11 specifically explain why we become so afraid of it:

(T-13-III.10:1) You who prefer separation to sanity cannot obtain it in your right mind.

One could easily substitute the word *specialness* here for *separation*, even though special relationships have not yet been discussed in the text. That discussion does not begin until the middle of Chapter 15, but Jesus is leading up to it, and he does talk here about special favor. Implied in this passage is that if we want to be separate and special, we must block off our right minds. This explains why we are always judging, finding fault, and continually indulging ourselves in special relationships—love or hate—and why we continue to wrestle with problems, experiencing conflict and guilt along the way. In the end, all problems are made up, but made to serve the specific purpose of keeping us from our right minds.

41

Therefore, if your goal is to maintain separation and retain your individuality, to keep yourself special and away from the Love of God—in the presence of which your specialness disappears—you must block out the Holy Spirit. As we will see again in a later reading, we accomplish this by listening only to the voice of specialness, in all its forms: despair, anger, hurt, excitement, conflict, problems, and dependency.

(10:2-3) You were at peace until you asked for special favor. And God did not give it for the request was alien to Him, and you could not ask this of a Father Who truly loved His Son.

This is what I described earlier—by taking the tiny, mad idea seriously after it seemed to arise in our minds, we recognized our separate existence: a self and consciousness that experienced itself in relationship to God. We looked at God, yet He did not see us; did not even know about us. That is when we sought special favor. We demanded that God pay attention to us, because if He did, that would mean we truly existed. If He did not, that would mean we do not. Very simple. But the Love of God knows only the perfect Oneness that is Itself. It does not know of separation, differentiation, uniqueness, and individuality. Therefore, if He were to grant our request, He would no longer be God—the One—and we would no longer be one with Him as His Son. We would have become the son of specialness, which in the dream we did.

(10:4) Therefore you made of Him an unloving father, demanding of Him what only such a father could give.

An unloving father can give only special love, which is of course special hate in disguise. In these few short sentences we find a summary of the ego story I talked about earlier, wherein God becomes the heavy—unloving, cruel, and withholding from us the love we need. What kind of loving father is that? All I wanted was a little hug and He refused to give it to me, not even acknowledging my existence. Therefore, to hell with Him! I call Him bad names and run away from home, calling back to Him, saying: "What you won't give me I will find elsewhere!" And indeed we do. We make up a self and a world, and then find the special attention, favors, and love we want—all of which prove that we exist, *without God.*

In the end, from the ego's point of view, it does not matter whether you love or hate me, approve or disapprove, are kind or betray and abandon me. As long as you do something to *me*, my ego is happy. Thus, while I wallow in the self-pity of yet another rejection, abandonment, betrayal, or loss, there is a part of me that jumps for joy, saying: "I've done it again, proving my existence for which someone else is responsible!" And so if it is not my unloving Father in Heaven Who has victimized me and made me suffer, it is my unloving spouse, child, parent, friend, boss—whoever, *but it is not me*! Yet I never allow any of this duplicity into awareness.

Whatever we believe we did to God, we do to everyone, because it is all the same. Whatever I believe you have done to me is what I believe I have done to you, because that is what I believe I did to God. It is all the same. That is why we do not have to heal our relationship with God directly. If we focus on forgiving where we believe our bodies are now, in our special relationships, that will heal everything.

(10:5) And the peace of God's Son was shattered, for he no longer understood his Father.

How can I be at peace when I think my Father is unloving and cruel, and that He is not only withholding love from me, but is now punishing me for having taken it from Him? How unfair! I had to take it from Him because He would not give it to me. I needed love and He refused it. I needed attention and approval and He withheld it. I therefore had no choice but to take it for myself. He is the cause of my problem, and now I am to be punished. How unfair! Thus we have to erect massive defenses against His punitive Love—the purpose of the world and all its special relationships.

Over and over and over again we repeat what we, as one Son, acted out with God. Peace is no longer possible, for war has become the reality. As long as we believe we are separate, as long as we believe we need something from others, there must be war and conflict. We will believe that what we need was rightfully ours before it was taken from us. Now we must seduce, cajole, and, manipulate for it—anything to retrieve what we so deeply believe is ours. And we resent having to beg, borrow, or steal to get it back. However, even more deeply buried is the thought it really was not ours in the first place; we stole it. Guilt quickly mixes with hate, and we have an absolute mess on our hands— the goal of all specialness.

(10:6) He [God's Son] **feared what he had made, but still more did he fear his real Father, having attacked his own glorious equality with Him.**

Our "glorious equality" with God is our oneness with Him, which we attacked by seeing ourselves as separate. We are now afraid of the cruel, unloving God we made, behind which lurks our fear of the *true* God, because we feel so guilty about our attack and the specialness we stole. Even more deeply buried is the fear that if we were in the presence of God's Love we would *not* be destroyed, but loved. That would mean there was no sin, no attack—nothing. *That* is our worst fear.

A later section called "The Forgiveness of Specialness" ends with the line: "Forgive your Father it was not His Will that you be crucified" (T-24.III.8:13). What we hold against God—what seems so impossible to forgive—is that He is *not* angry; He is not the cruel, unloving, and vengeful father we made up. As long as we see Him that way we are fine, because, as we have seen, He is noticing us. His paying attention to us—even in anger—demonstrates our existence, which demonstrates in turn that we accomplished the impossible and achieved our separation. What our egos cannot forgive Him for is that He does *not* crucify us, which He cannot do because He does not see any sin. It was not His Will His Son be crucified, by whatever name you call him, and if indeed it was not His Will, everything the ego has told us is a lie.

Again, if Othello had really explored what was going on, he would have realized he was not being crucified by his wife or one of his best friends. Only Iago—symbol of the ego—was betraying him. There was thus a part of Othello's mind, which is part of everyone's mind, that luxuriated in the pain of being unfairly treated. We all know the line: "Beware of the temptation to perceive yourself unfairly treated" (T-26.X.4:1). If God is not angry and cruel, none of what we believe or perceive is real, which means *we* are not real, either. That is our fear, and what we hold against God. We *need* Him to be an abuser. This means, of course, that Othello needed Iago, just as Iago needed Othello; a victim requires a victimizer—partners in crime, as it were. Indeed, you could not think of the play without thinking of both Othello *and* Iago.

(11:1-2) In peace [the peace of Heaven] **he needed nothing and asked for nothing. In war he demanded everything and found nothing.**

The only thing we can ever find that has value is love. And love does not exist on a battleground. Love sees everyone as one, but the ego turned our minds into a battleground: God against us. Since *ideas leave not their source*, the world that arose from the mind's battleground is also a battleground: dog-eat-dog; kill or be killed; *one or the other.* How, then, is peace possible? Peace comes only when there is no perception of separate interests, and no needs to intrude upon the love that unites us with one another, as this passage from the text makes clear:

> In the holy instant no one is special, for your personal needs intrude on no one to make your brothers seem different. Without the values from the past, you would see them all the same and like yourself. Nor would you see any separation between yourself and them (T-15.V.8:2-4).

(11:3) For how could the gentleness of love respond to his [the Son's] **demands, except by departing in peace and returning to the Father?**

Jesus is saying here that the moment we chose specialness, love was gone from our awareness. The only way it can be recovered is to choose its reflection here on earth, which we see when we no longer perceive anyone else's interests as separate from our own—the bottom line, the essence of forgiveness. If I have needs that only you can meet, our interests are different. I have a need, and all I care about is that you give me what I want: attention, money, approval, recognition, physical pleasure—whatever it is I think I need from you. But there is no joining here, for there is no caring, no shared interests; only what *you* can give *me*.

Real love, and its reflection here as the shared interests of the Sonship, can do nothing except remain where it is. It cannot respond to our demands for specialness; It simply waits for us to come to it. You may recall the line: "Love waits on welcome, not on time...." (T-13.VII.9:7). All that is needed is for us to invite love in, done by asking Jesus to help us perceive our special love or hate partner as no different from ourselves. That is the simplicity of *A Course in Miracles*—everything is perceived as the same, governed by the one principle of forgiveness.

(11:4) If the Son did not wish to remain in peace, he could not remain at all.

I cannot be in Heaven on *my* terms; only on God's terms—the state of perfect Oneness, love, and peace, which is reflected here by our perception of shared interests. As is said in the manual for teachers, all we need do to establish ourselves as a teacher of God is not see another's interests as separate from our own (M-1.1:1-2). It is instructive to look around you—your personal world and the world at large—and see how the world operates in the exact opposite fashion. Everyone's needs are separate from everyone else's, at the personal and collective levels. That is why we have interpersonal conflicts and wars between nations. We do not realize our inherent sameness as separated selves; we are all in the same miserable ego boat together.

(11:5-7) For a darkened mind cannot live in the light, and it must seek a place of darkness where it can believe it is where it is not. God did not allow this to happen. Yet you demanded that it happen, and therefore believed that it was so.

These extremely important lines go to the heart of the ego thought system. From a different point of view, we hate God because He does not play our game. He remains where He is, because He cannot be anywhere else; *there is nowhere else.* And so we are continually attempting to drag Him into the world; and, as students of *A Course in Miracles*, we continually attempt to drag it and Jesus into the world. We want things fixed here, as if there were a "here" in which to have things fixed. And so nothing really is. We cannot ask God and Jesus for help on our terms, for that would make Them allies of our specialness. Yet we persist in asking for help with our made-up problems, while the only problem is our having chosen to listen to the wrong voice, as did Othello. This is why, again, the play is so problematic for its audience. Each of us is secretly an Othello, and we are terrified of the disastrous consequences of choosing to listen to the "honest" voice of specialness, ending up destroying what we love most. This point cannot be emphasized often enough.

There is a wonderful passage in the text where Jesus says you cannot approach God's altar with condemnation in your heart. The Creator's altar is the oneness of perfect love, and if you condemn anyone—exclude *anyone* from the Sonship—you cannot approach His altar, and you will believe the door has been barred. However, we are the ones who have barred the door, not God. Here is the passage:

Christ is at God's altar, waiting to welcome His Son. But come wholly without condemnation, for otherwise you will believe that the door is barred and you cannot enter. The door is not barred, and it is impossible that you cannot enter the place where God would have you be. But love yourself with the Love of Christ, for so does your Father love you. You can refuse to enter, but you cannot bar the door that Christ holds open. Come unto me who hold it open for you, for while I live it cannot be shut, and I live forever. God is my life and yours, and nothing is denied by God to His Son (T-11.IV.6).

Thus, even though Jesus holds the door open for us, we have to go to him, bringing our darkness to his light. However, as we shall now see, when we want to remain separated from him, we bring the light to the darkness: "For a darkened mind cannot live in the light, and it must seek a place of darkness where it can believe it is where it is not." What supports the subterfuge of believing we are where we are not is bringing Jesus there. If he is in the world's darkness of sin and separation, we must be there, too. *But Jesus is not there.* It is only a trick of our specialness that he is. This passage describes how we asked God to play our specialness game and notice us. As we have seen, He did not because He could not, and thus began the ego's dream that we accepted as reality. We demanded that separation happen so we could be special, and so believed that it did. Our projected image of God justified and reinforced what we thought occurred in the separation, but in truth nothing did.

Jesus repeats his point in Chapter 16, in the context of our special relationships:

(T-16.V.4:1) It is in the special relationship, born of the hidden wish for special love from God, that the ego's hatred triumphs.

My special relationships are born of the hidden wish for special love from God. Therefore, when I get special love from someone else, I am thumbing my nose in God's face, saying: "You see? You would not give me what I needed, so I found someone who would." That someone, then, becomes my God. Jesus reiterates this same idea later in this section: "If you perceived the special relationship as a triumph over God, would you want it?" (T-16.V.10:1). Every time I get what I want from you, I have triumphed over you. In thus getting what I want—love, attention, approval, admiration—I am secretly acting out my triumph over God. Jesus is helping us realize that this is what we are doing, and to have us ask ourselves in earnest whether it is truly what we want.

The pain everyone feels at the end of the play is that Othello recognizes what he is giving up. His guilt impels him to follow his course of action even though he is aware of what he is losing. Secretly, we all believe we would not be able to stop ourselves from destroying what we love, and in the process prevent ourselves from having the true peace and love for which we all yearn. Our pain at the play's conclusion comes from our inner recognition that we are like Othello, perhaps not as dramatic in consequence, but certainly in desire.

(4:2) For the special relationship is the renunciation of the Love of God, and the attempt to secure for the self the specialness that He denied.

Here again, one could not ask for a more explicit statement of what the world is about. Everything here is based on special relationships, and therefore everything here represents our renunciation of God's Love, telling Him we have taken care of our own needs and wants. Our lives represent the determination to get for our separated selves the specialness He denied us; and when we feel the pain of yet another failed relationship—Othello's *"Chaos is come again"* (III,iii,92)—we bring our painful chaos to God, self-righteously saying: "This is all Your fault. If only You had paid attention to me I would not have left home, foresworn love, and embarked on this futile search for special relationships, all ending with pain, more pain, and still more pain. It is all Your doing."

This is a set-up—to be tempted by the cherished perception of unfair treatment. Again: "Beware of the temptation to perceive yourself unfairly treated" (T-26.X.4:1). We love to keep ourselves in the darkness because the light is so threatening to our special self.

(4:3-4) It is essential to the preservation of the ego that you believe this specialness is not hell, but Heaven. For the ego would never have you see that separation could only be loss, being the one condition in which Heaven could not be.

The only way the ego can continue to survive is to have us believe that specialness is Heaven. Remember—the ego is our self that wants to be an autonomous individual, and that wants to be separate from love and from our Source. It is essential to the ego that we believe specialness is wonderful. Needless to say, when a special love relationship works, we feel it is Heaven; and when it does not work—which inevitably happens—we feel we have been thrust into hell.

One could say that the purpose of *A Course in Miracles* is to learn that specialness is hell, not Heaven. It is hell because it is *ex*clusive, not *in*clusive. As long as you have a need, you cannot be happy unless some specific event occurs, unless you are with a certain person, living in a certain place, having a certain job, a certain amount of money, a certain kind of car, your children have a certain success, your body behaves in a certain way, and so on. As long as you believe you have specific needs, you will never have the peace of God and remember Heaven. Remember, Heaven is a state of perfect and non-dualistic Oneness:

> The Kingdom of Heaven is the dwelling place of the Son of God, who left not his Father and dwells not apart from Him. Heaven is not a place nor a condition. It is merely an awareness of perfect Oneness, and the knowledge that there is nothing else; nothing outside this Oneness, and nothing else within (T-18.VI.1:4-6).

Heaven is a state of completion, not by anything external but by the acceptance of God's Love. Thus, *A Course in Miracles* is about understanding the true nature of specialness, and what it is you are choosing against in order to have it. At some point you must recognize the tremendous pain involved in seeking the ego's promises of completion, for it would never have you see that separation can only mean loss.

Specialness, separation, exclusion, *one or the other*—these always involve loss, and what we are truly losing is the Love of God. Later in the text there is the section "The 'Sacrifice' of Oneness" (T-26.I). Note that the word *sacrifice* is in quotes. We believe we are sacrificing Oneness in order to be special, and it is imperative we become aware of what we are throwing away, for only then can we choose again. Othello clearly sees at the end what he is losing, knowing how much he loves what he is murdering, and yet he does it anyway. To state this one more time, our stomachs churn because we see what we secretly would do, too. Here we are, devoted students of *A Course in Miracles*, and yet we do the exact opposite of what Jesus teaches us. That is the fear this play elicits in its audience: We, like Othello, would choose against love. Othello murdered the one he truly loved, and whom he loved even as he

49

was murdering her. We love this Course, which is solely about giving up judgment, and yet we still find ourselves judging—even as we read, study, and attend workshops on the Course. Just imagine the guilt—pledging to give up judgment, and still judging! But we are not really in touch with the depths of our duplicity, and so we are continually driven to judge.

There is a telling line where Othello exclaims to Iago: "*But yet, the pity of it, Iago! O Iago, the pity of it, Iago!*" (IV,i,196); cried out when he believes what Iago wants him to think is going on: "*the pity of it.*" What happens with us here *is* pitiful! What we do is terrible, and our problem is that we do not know we are doing it. We truly believe we can get away with judging and hating others, finding fault with them and reinforcing separation. We truly think we can get away with indulging our specialness, still believing we can be happy and peaceful living the lie. In *A Course in Miracles* Jesus exposes this lie of self-deception. He has us look squarely at the ego—our Iago—and tells us: "It is not honest. Do not listen to a word it says. It may seem truthful, and the world may think its thought system is true, but it is not." *Look at what your ego is doing*, Jesus tells us in Chapter 17; look at the picture, not the frame (T-17.IV). Look at the ego's picture of death. *Look at it*. Do not let the frame, aglitter with diamonds and rubies, hide the picture from your sight. *Look at the picture.* Look at what your specialness is offering you and realize what you are settling for. See what you are losing by choosing the ego's lie that you will get what you truly want, and still be happy.

What *will* happen when you listen to the lie is that you will become more and more comfortable in the darkness; so much so that after a while you will forget about the light entirely. Then you will be in Othello's shoes when he says "*Put out the light,*" as he is about to extinguish permanently the light of his love. Recall that in looking at her he says "*I know not where is that Promethean heat that can thy light relume*" (V,ii,12)—he knows he will never recover the light once he puts it out. That, once again, is our secret fear: We will become so enamored of the darkened guilt of our specialness we will forget the light, forever losing what we love.

Let me say a few more words about this so we do not miss the gentleness of Jesus' teaching and guidance. In one sense, every time we take a breath we are being Othello. But we need to keep a reasonable perspective. Jesus is not saying we should not breathe, eat, drink, have sex, accumulate wealth, etc., but he is asking us, whatever we do, to try not to do it without him. This means, if we are going to do it *with* him, everyone else will be there, too. We then realize: "Yes, I am breathing and that keeps my illusory and love-limiting body going. But everyone else is breathing, too, which means everyone is the same." Thus does breathing become a holy relationship, because with this new under-standing—the vision of Christ—we are not seeing differences. It may be easy to accept that everyone is the same because everyone breathes and eats, but it may not be as easy to accept that everyone is the same because everyone hates, indulges specialness, and worships at its blood-drenched altar. Both the good and bad judge, criticize, and believe they live in a world of separate interests. Thus we begin with what originally had the effect of reinforcing the body as a witness to separation, but then see a different purpose for it: learning everyone is the same. Our perceptions change accordingly, and breathing—which represents *all* human experience—becomes part of the Holy Spirit's happy dream, instead reminding us of the ego's guilt.

Silencing the Voice of the Holy Spirit

We now turn to "The Treachery of Specialness" in Chapter 24, which addresses the ego's counsel that we continue to worship at its shrine of specialness and hear its voice of *one or the other.* We begin with paragraph 3, another of those passages in *A Course in Miracles* that are unmistakable in their meaning; its point being that specialness is purposive. We want to be involved in a special relationship—whether love or hate, pleasure or pain—because that keeps us out of our right minds. We *want* to stay in the darkness, enshrouded in guilt's shadows, terrified of the light in which our individual selves do not exist. To this end we want relationships that are problematic and con-flicted, glorious and depressing—reaching both the heights and depths. We love their drama because that ensures we will never hear the Holy Spirit, never go to our right minds and thus never return home. We want to believe that Heaven can be found on earth when our specialness needs are met. However, the resultant guilt is enormous, for each time we choose specialness we are again thumbing our noses in God's face, not to mention the faces of the Holy Spirit and Jesus. Guilt continues, reinforcing itself. The more guilt that is unrecognized and therefore unhealed, the more it is projected, trapping us in the seemingly endless cycle of guilt and attack.

(T-24.II.3:1) Specialness is the idea of sin made real.

We have seen that the idea of sin is the idea of separating from God, which takes the form in our myth of demanding special favor, to which God does not respond. Since *ideas leave not their source*, the thought of sin remains in our minds, from which it is projected. We then live it out with everyone in our dream, but now it seems very real in its variegated forms of specialness.

(3:2) Sin is impossible even to imagine without this base.

Sin needs specialness because that is its source, which is nothing more than separation and differentiation. Specialness leads to neediness, which makes demands that lead to experiences of pleasure or pain, depending on whether or not the needs are met.

(3:3) For sin arose from it, out of nothingness; an evil flower with no roots at all.

What established Iago as evil was Othello's listening to him. This is similar to passages later in the text where Jesus explains that it takes two people to make a sickness: one who complains of symptoms, and the other who makes them real by reacting to them (see, for example, T-28.III.2). This does not mean you do not help someone who is sick. At issue here is not form or behavior, but the content in our minds: for instance, when someone else's symptoms affect you adversely, or make you happy. Once affected, you make sickness and the body real, and therefore the ego as well. Similarly, just as it takes two to make a sickness, it takes two to make evil: one who commits it, and one who experiences its effects. Yet just as the source of sickness—the thought of separation—is nothing, so is the source of sin—the ego thought system. Despite its bluster, the ego can never leave its source in nothingness.

(3:4) Here is the self-made "savior," the "creator" who creates unlike the Father, and which made His Son like to itself and not like unto Him.

In my earlier discussion of the Gnostic myth of Sophia I mentioned that her mistake was in trying to create like her Father. She could not do so because she was not the Source. This led to her abortion, the

Gnostic term for the afterbirth. That "residue" or "miscreation" was solidified by her grief and guilt. This eventually led to the world and the being who made the world, called Ialdabaoth in some Gnostic systems, a corruption of the biblical names of God, and who, in effect, is Sophia's son. The point here is that the cosmos, including the body, came from the guilt over trying to create like God—usurping His role as Creator—and not being able to do so.

(3:5-6) His "special" sons are many, never one, each one in exile from himself, and Him of Whom they are a part. Nor do they love the Oneness which created them as one with Him.

How can you love the Oneness that created you at one with Him when you want to be an individual? How can you love this Course, whose purpose is to restore in you the awareness of that Oneness, when you still want your specialness and to be recognized by Jesus as a specific self? when you want to pick up the "phone" and say to him: "Hey, I have a problem. Please help me."? That is what we want and demand. And therefore we think we are actually picking up a mental phone and calling the Holy Spirit, believing we are hearing His Voice and having our specific needs met. We do not understand the tremendous power of our unconscious investment in the ego, and therefore do not realize we are listening to our own voice. God's Voice does not really answer specifically—nor does Jesus, the Holy Spirit's manifestation—but with the abstract love that is His essence, the one Self. This love is a non-specific presence in our minds, but as long as we think we are in this world, our experience will be that specific answers are heard. But these words or symbols are not from God or His Voice, but from our minds, which automatically translate non-specific, abstract love into some form related to our needs and experiences here. Our response to that need will then be whatever is most loving and all-inclusive under the circumstances, embracing everyone in its healing love, without exception.

Our job, then, is simply to get our egos out of the way, which we do by bringing the darkness of our ego's specialness to the light of Jesus' love. But Othello, who represents all of us, instead of bringing the darkness of Iago's lies to Desdemona's truth and asking her what was going on, did exactly the opposite. He brought her love and truth to Iago's lies. He confronted her with accusations. That is the difference between bringing the light to the darkness, which is what the ego wants, and bringing the darkness to the light, which is what Jesus asks us to do. All we are asked in *A Course in Miracles* is to have a "little willingness" to look at what our egos are doing. Looking with Jesus means recognizing the tremendous cost of our specialness, the price we pay for our neediness. This involves the genuine recognition that we believe, as Iago says in his Credo, that there is no hope or love here, and God's cruelty makes death our inevitable fate. Everyone lies, for we are but actors on a stage, secretly believing that Iago's creed is the truth because that is what we believe is our truth. This is the play we must look at; and only when we look at our specialness without guilt and fear will the light that is just behind the darkness shine through. Everything in our perception will then change.

(3:7) They chose their specialness instead of Heaven and instead of peace, and wrapped it carefully in sin, to keep it "safe" from truth.

That is what we all did, why we are so guilty and always sabotaging ourselves by the same specialness that drove Othello to such insane behavior. We chose specialness instead of the peace of Heaven, and wrapped it carefully in sin, protected by guilt. Thus was truth kept away from sin, and that is why we must bring our specialness to love (the ego to the Holy Spirit) and not love to specialness (the Holy Spirit to the ego).

Jesus is now quite specific about the consequences of having chosen specialness:

(4:1) You are not special.

No one likes to hear those words. Realize what they mean! You are not an individual, autonomous and independent, but part of God's living and loving Oneness; no different from anyone else in the world. This is quite different from specialness, which is predicated on differences for it always involves comparisons: "You are more special to me than anyone else"; "This is the most special gift I have ever received." When Jesus says "You are not special," he is not denying our obvious differences in form, but speaking only of the sameness of our content. In fact, earlier in the text he speaks of the special relationship as the triumph of form over content (T-16.V.12:1-5). Specialness thus cannot be the truth, for there are no true differences among God's Sons. If we are the same, then we cannot justify our judgments and accusations;

nor our attack thoughts, criticisms, and fault-finding; neither can we justify our hatred of God for not granting us special favor.

(4:2) If you think you are, and would defend your specialness against the truth of what you really are, how can you know the truth?

If you think *A Course in Miracles* does not work; if you say you have tried and tried but still have not had the experience of oneness that it seems to promise, *read this sentence again.* If you say you do not understand love and truth, and do not feel yourself getting any closer to it, *read this sentence again.* How could you possibly allow yourself to experience the truth when you are afraid of it, and seek always to defend against it? As long as you believe you are here and different from everyone else, you must be defending against the truth of our inherent oneness as God's one Son.

(4:3) What answer that the Holy Spirit gives can reach you, when it is your specialness to which you listen, and which asks and answers?

When you ask Jesus to meet your specific needs, it is your specialness that will answer. Abstract, non-specific love cannot answer in specifics because it would then stop being what it is. How can you hear the Holy Spirit "when it is your specialness to which you listen," when it is your specialness that asks for help and then answers?

(4:4) Its tiny answer, soundless in the melody that pours from God to you eternally in loving praise of what you are, is all you listen to.

This is another way of saying that the bottom line for us is fear: the terror that our specialness would disappear if we let ourselves hear the Holy Spirit's melody, the "song of prayer." And, because of the principle of *one or the other,* it would. The following excerpt from "The Fear of Redemption" underscores this important teaching:

> You have built your whole insane belief system because you think you would be helpless in God's Presence, and you would save yourself from His Love because you think it would crush you into nothingness. You are afraid it would sweep you away from yourself and make you little, because you believe that magnitude lies in defiance, and that attack is grandeur. You think you have made a

world God would destroy; and by loving Him, which you do, you would throw this world away, which you *would*. Therefore, you have used the world to cover your love, and the deeper you go into the blackness of the ego's foundation, the closer you come to the Love that is hidden there. *And it is this that frightens you....* Your individual death seems more valuable than your living oneness, for what is given you is not so dear as what you made. You are more afraid of God than of the ego, and love cannot enter where it is not welcome (T-13.III.4;5:3-4).

This cogently explains why we choose to hear the wrong voice, and why we choose to murder, whether we do it literally, as did Othello, or figuratively, as we all do—murdering love by the worship of special-ness. We are terrified, again, that if we let ourselves hear love's melody we will disappear; our individual selves vanishing in the presence of even the faintest hint of the "forgotten song," which sings to us of shared interests in place of the separate interests of the world.

(4:5-6) And that vast song of honor and of love for what you are seems silent and unheard before its "mightiness." You strain your ears to hear its soundless voice, and yet the Call of God Himself is soundless to you.

Mightiness is in quotation marks because Jesus is talking about spe-cialness. We strain to hear a voice that does not exist because we are ter-rified of the Voice that does. The "Call of God Himself" is in our minds as the Holy Spirit, the memory of Who we are as Christ; the link that returns us home and which resides in everyone. Yet we consistently embrace specialness in order to drown out that Voice. We become angry, find fault, feel sorry for ourselves, and on and on—all part of the ego's subtle plot to ensnare us in its web, just as Iago ensnared Othello in his. Remember, Iago ensnared Othello because of his rage over Othello's having chosen against him. Cassio's appointment was its symbol, for Iago was really punishing Othello for his having chosen love, the light over darkness. Iago thus saw to it that Othello would never again make that choice by seducing him into identifying with his lies, the ego's plan for all of us. To ensure that we never choose against light over darkness, love over hate, we are continually seduced into the ego's web of specialness. Choosing to believe its lies, we do not hear the call of truth, that "vast song of honor and of love."

(5:1-4) You can defend your specialness, but never will you hear the Voice for God beside it. They speak a different language and they fall on different ears. To every special one a different message, and one with different meaning, is the truth. Yet how can truth be different to each one?

The first law of chaos is that there is a hierarchy of illusions, truth is relative (T-23.II.2:1-3)—the sophist argument that Socrates countered in his wise logic. Both Socrates and Plato taught the absolute nature of truth, as does Jesus in *A Course in Miracles*. How can the truth be different for different people, when all are part of perfect Oneness? Expressions of truth may take different forms, but truth is true, for it is one.

(5:5) The special messages the special hear convince them they are different and apart; each in his special sins and "safe" from love, which does not see his specialness at all.

That is what enrages us. Love does not see our specialness, for how can it know what does not exist? This of course is the ultimate insult to our egos: God does not know about separation and specialness, so He cannot know about us as individuals. Stated another way, because love is abstract and non-specific, it cannot see the specificity of specialness; love and specialness are mutually exclusive, as are Oneness and separation.

(5:6) Christ's vision is their "enemy," for it sees not what they would look upon, and it would show them that the specialness they think they see is an illusion.

Christ's vision is part of the illusion, but it is a forgiving, right-minded one. It sees everyone as the same, and that explains why we do not ask Jesus for real help. His answer to a genuine request is vision: everyone and every situation is the same, for no perception of differences is ever justified. Again, this is not about form, but content. To requote this important statement from the text: "Nothing so blinding as perception of form" (T-22.III.6:7). Eyes perceive differences at the level of form, and that is why they deceive. Christ's vision, on the other hand, comes from the content of truth's reflection that sees past form to the oneness of mind and spirit; beyond differences to the underlying sameness of God's Son. Lesson 151 nicely summarizes vision's gift to us through the Holy Spirit:

He [the Voice for God] will not tell you that your brother should be judged by what your eyes behold in him, nor what his body's mouth says to your ears, nor what your fingers' touch reports of him. He passes by such idle witnesses, which merely bear false witness to God's Son.... He gives you vision which can look beyond these grim appearances, and can behold the gentle face of Christ in all of them.... And you will see the love beyond the hate, the constancy in change, the pure in sin, and only Heaven's blessing on the world.... In everyone and everything His Voice would speak to you of nothing but your Self and your Creator, Who is one with Him. So will you see the holy face of Christ in everything, and hear in everything no sound except the echo of God's Voice (W-pI.151.7:2-3; 10:2; 11:3; 12:3-4)

(6) What would they see instead? The shining radiance of the Son of God, so like his Father that the memory of Him springs instantly to mind. And with this memory, the Son remembers his own creations, as like to him as he is to his Father. And all the world he made, and all his specialness, and all the sins he held in its defense against himself, will vanish as his mind accepts the truth about himself, as it returns to take their place. This is the only "cost" of truth: You will no longer see what never was, nor hear what makes no sound. Is it a sacrifice to give up nothing, and to receive the Love of God forever?

That is our basic choice; all we are asked to do. The miracle's only purpose is to have us see this choice: "Who with the Love of God upholding him could find the choice of miracles or murder hard to make?" (T-23.IV.9:8). Who could find it difficult to choose between Desdemona's Heaven and Iago's hell? No one, unless God's Love were pushed away because the Iagos of the world were deemed more attractive than its Desdemonas; unless the shadow of guilt were preferable to "the shining radiance of the Son of God." Only when we see clearly the hell to which worshipping at the altar of specialness brought us can we choose Heaven's forgiveness, allowing Christ's vision to penetrate the veils of specialness and reveal the Love of God that is God's Son, our true Self.

Asking for Specifics

Before moving to the third part of our exploration of the ego, I return to the theme of asking the Holy Spirit for specifics, as it continues to be a source of confusion and frustration for many students of a *A Course in Miracles*. Some readers might be inclined to take my earlier comments to mean that asking for specifics is incompatible with being a "good" student. To address that adequately would require a full workshop and a couple of books, which I have already written,[7] but I will highlight here some of the more important aspects of this important issue.

First, there is a specific reason (pardon the pun) this issue returns again and again, and it probably comes as a surprise to most of us. If I ask for specific things, that means I am a specific person. It means a specific Jesus is specifically involved with my specific needs, and will grant my specific requests with specific answers: specifics, specifics, specifics. But the Love of God, being formless and abstract, is *non-specific*. How better, then, to defend against the non-specific, abstract Love of God than to demand that God (or His representatives) meet my specific needs? It is a perfect way of *not* bringing the darkness to the light; of *not* bringing my specifics to the non-specific. Instead, I bring the non-specific to the specific, thereby making It specific and preserving my specific self.

That is why everyone loves the early Helen stories that appear in my book *Absence from Felicity*—the story of Jesus helping her find the winter Borgana coat she wanted, for example (pp. 230-31)—and they choose to ignore the later ones. People need to continue with the rest of the book, because what follows these accounts of Helen's asking for specifics corrects Helen's early tendency to ask Jesus for help with very specific problems. Our scribe was very psychic and, as the manual says, these abilities can serve the ego or the Holy Spirit, depending on their purpose (M-25). When her fear of his non-specific love diminished somewhat, Jesus essentially asked Helen to move beyond *her* form of asking, and adopt *his*. This entailed, for example, not asking him to tell her what specifically to say to someone, but rather to ask his

---

7. See for example, *The Message of A Course in Miracles*, Vol. Two: *Few Choose to Listen*, Chapter 4; *Absence from Felicity*, Chapter 17; "The Song of Prayer" – audio tape album.

help in seeing that person through the eyes of peace rather than judgment (pp. 381-82).

In my book (p. 427) I describe an incident that happened when Helen and I left the Medical Center early one afternoon. It was a lovely, spring day and I asked: "Where do you want to go shopping?" because that is what we usually did on spring afternoons. But this time Helen replied: "It said, I do not have to do that any more." ("It" was Helen's euphemism for "Jesus" or "he.") From that point on we did not go shopping unless it was for some specific things that Helen truly needed, rather than shop as a distraction. As I explain later in the book, Jesus did not literally speak to her (see Chapter 17). Helen's experience of his voice in this instance reflected her readiness to let go of one of her favorite defenses. Shopping—going from one store to the next—was one of Helen's ways of keeping Jesus at arms length. For instance, she was a master at buying shoes that did not fit, which meant that the following week she would have to return to the store to exchange them. There is the now famous story about how Helen and I once spent a full afternoon looking for green panty hose, when it was obvious that our expedition was set up from the beginning to fail. Therefore, hearing: "You do not have to do this any more" was really Helen herself saying: "I do not have to continue this defense, because I am no longer so afraid of love's presence in my mind. Thus one should not stop with the story about Helen's Borgana coat from Klein's Bargain Basement. Rather, that experience should be seen in the context of her gradually and gently coming to terms with Jesus as he really was. Jesus further pointed out to Helen that continually asking him for specifics was attempting, out of fear, to "manage the unmanageable" —his love, which cannot be managed—by translating it into a specific form.

There is nothing that says you cannot ask the Holy Spirit for whatever you want. Just do not expect Him to give it to you, because—one more time—He does not know about specific things. When we think the Holy Spirit is answering our specific requests, we are not in touch with the fact that *we* are the ones who are both asking and answering. The pamphlet *The Song of Prayer* was written precisely for the purpose of helping us learn not to ask the Holy Spirit and Jesus for specific things. Let me read from its first chapter, which should help clarify this point:

(S-1.I.2:1-2) You have been told to ask the Holy Spirit for the answer to any specific problem, and that you will receive a specific answer if such is your need. You have also been told that there is only one problem and one answer.

There are relatively few passages in *A Course in Miracles* that say what is in this first sentence, but there is no question they do appear. The second statement is more common. But after reading the two together, one would naturally think that something strange is going on. If there is only one problem and one answer, then the problem of separation and its answer of Atonement must be non-specific. On the other hand, Jesus is also saying we can ask for specific things. Anticipating this concern, he says:

(2:3) In prayer this is not contradictory.

As the pamphlet explains, prayer is a *process*. Indeed, the very next section is called "The Ladder of Prayer." Thus, if we were to think of our spiritual journey with *A Course in Miracles* as analogous to climbing a ladder, then its bottom is where we believe we are as bodies. But by having chosen the right teacher we are at last on the right ladder. This teacher is still thought of as a body; a spiritual body, perhaps, or an etheric one, but nonetheless a specific person with whom we relate, such as Jesus. The top of the ladder represents the real world—when the Atonement has been accepted once and for all—in which there are no specifics. And beyond the ladder is Heaven itself.

A Course in Miracles helps us ascend the ladder. We begin at the bottom, where we think we are, as bodies relating with other bodies, asking for specific help. The passages in question meet us at this level. As we make our way up the ladder, however, we begin to understand there is really only one thing we need—forgiveness. You may recall a line early in the text that says "the only meaningful prayer is for forgiveness, because those who have been forgiven have everything" (T-3.V.6:3). Since we already have everything, we need only to forgive—let go of our guilt—so that we remember that we indeed do have everything. Thus, when Jesus says "in prayer, this is not contradictory" he is saying: "I am talking to you out of both sides of my mouth because you think there are two sides of *your* mouth; and until you realize you have only *one* side—in fact you do not even have a mouth—we are going to pretend." There are many passages in *A Course in Miracles* in which Jesus essentially tells us he is pretending—speaking to us in symbols that are not meant to be taken literally—but this is how he must speak to us; otherwise we will not understand him.

Jesus' point is that at the beginning of the process we do ask for specific things, because that is how we learn he is our friend and not our enemy. He does not seek to punish or crucify us, or demand sacrifice. However, as we make our way up the ladder we begin to lose interest in the specifics, because we want the experience of love more and more. We grow tired of hearing only little hints of melody—a few harmonies, overtones, and echoes here and there. We want the song itself. All the Holy Spirit and Jesus give us is love. All that God is, is love. And so he asks us:

> Can this [the remembrance of God] be traded for a bit of trifling advice about a problem of an instant's duration? God answers only for eternity. But still all little answers are contained in this (S-1.I.4:6-8).

Once you have experienced that love, you automatically know the most loving response for all situations. That does not mean you do not do things in the world. It means only that you do not do them out of *need*. You will make decisions; we all make decisions. But you will make a decision that is loving, meaning a decision that will hurt no one. There is no sense of opposition, and therefore no anger or guilt. What remains is the extension of love to all members of the Sonship— not in form, but in content.

Jesus uses the extremely helpful analogy of a ladder because it reminds us, again, that this is a process, wherein we ascend step by step as we gradually overcome our fear of accepting responsibility for the condition of separation. Heretofore we sought to blame someone or something else, and feel we were merely robots—something that was acted on. The ego's little voice constantly warned that if we ever get back in touch with the power of our minds to choose, we will make the wrong choice again. Our guilt is so enormous that, rather than deal with it, we simply pretend none of it happened; we never heard of separation or had anything to do with it. We claim we are acting and feeling the way we do because of multitudinous things impinging on us. And so it is a process of reducing our fear, and we must learn to be patient with ourselves as we make our way home.

Guilt Demands Punishment – Self-Sabotage

The third part of our exploration of the ego is the idea that guilt demands punishment. This fundamental ego law leads us to sabotage ourselves, which was so apparent in the character of Othello. We begin with the section in the text called "The Ego's Use of Guilt," the third paragraph:

(T-5.V.3:1-2) The ego is the part of the mind that believes in division. How could part of God detach itself without believing it is attacking Him?

This is part of the ego's myth. In order to render us mindless, thereby ensuring that we would never change our minds, the ego makes up a story, just as Iago weaved his web of lies: a little snippet from here, a piece from there, a part from somewhere else, ending up with a picture that is the exact opposite of the truth. The ego tells us we detached ourselves from God, which means we attacked and killed Him. The ego drills into our minds that this is a serious sin, and this is what Jesus is referring to here.

(3:3-5) We spoke before of the authority problem as based on the concept of usurping God's power. The ego believes that this is what you did because it believes that it *is* you. If you identify with the ego, you must perceive yourself as guilty.

"Usurping God's power" is another definition of *sin*: God is not the Creator; I am. Needless to say, the decision-making part of our minds that identifies with the ego is very much drawn to its thought system of separation and specialness, sin and guilt. Notice that the title of this section is "The Ego's Use of Guilt." It is the first serious discussion in the text about guilt, which in the broadest sense is any negative feeling one has about oneself. Many discussions follow this in the text, wherein Jesus essentially speaks of the unholy trinity of *sin, guilt,* and *fear*—the core of the ego's myth.

(3:6) Whenever you respond to your ego you will experience guilt, and you will fear punishment.

When I identify with my ego I am choosing against the Holy Spirit's love, because the law of the split mind holds that if I am not with the ego I am with the Holy Spirit, and vice versa. I must be identified with one or the other, and cannot be identified with neither. If I choose to identify with the ego, it tells me I have sinned by again pushing love away, again crucifying Jesus, and again telling God His Love is not enough and so I will make my own. Because guilt demands punishment, and since my guilt tells me I have sinned, I must believe I deserve to be punished for what I have done.

(3:7-11) The ego is quite literally a fearful thought. However ridiculous the idea of attacking God may be to the sane mind, never forget that the ego is not sane. It represents a delusional system, and speaks for it. Listening to the ego's voice means that you believe it is possible to attack God, and that a part of Him has been torn away by you. Fear of retaliation from without follows, because the severity of the guilt is so acute that it must be projected.

In this one paragraph we have a summary of the ego thought system. I choose the ego, which tells me I have sinned by attacking God. It then urges me to protect my mind by projecting the guilt, and so I believe someone else will punish me for what I secretly believe I have done. Ultimately it would be God Who punishes since He was the object of my first sin, but I now act this out with everyone here: If I believe I did it with God, as we all do since we are one Son, then I must do it with everyone. I must believe that people are angry with me and will reject me. Why? Because I rejected them first.

Near the end of "The 'Dynamics' of the Ego" Jesus says, "If he speaks not of Christ to you, you spoke not of Christ to him" (T-11.V.18:6): If your brother is not speaking of Christ to you—if he is not kind or Christ-like—you were not kind or Christ-like to him. This does not mean that if you say something unkind to me it is because I actually behaved unkindly toward you. Rather, if I *perceive* you as not being Christ-like to me—unkind, judgmental, rejecting, etc.—it can only be because in my mind I first separated from you. This does not make me responsible for your ego behavior. Remember, perception is not what our eyes see or ears hear, but interpretation: how we *interpret* what we see and hear. If I perceive you attacking me rather than calling out for help—the Holy Spirit's interpretation—it can only be because I believe I attacked you first. If I did not act it out behaviorally, it was nonetheless in my mind. Otherwise, I would not take your ego behavior personally.

It could also be that you are not coming from your ego at all. I could be making the whole thing up. Othello would not have believed that Desdemona were unfaithful to him if he had not first accused himself of being unfaithful—not necessarily unfaithful to her—but to love. The issue is not what Desdemona has or has not done, and there are no indications in the play that she was unfaithful.

We can speculate that if Othello had been a student of *A Course in Miracles* he would have gone within to ask for help the minute Iago's poison began to work and the jealous and murderous feelings became aroused. He would have asked himself what he was accusing himself of. Then, regardless of what Desdemona was doing or not doing, he would have realized his anger was coming from his secret guilt over having betrayed love and, reacting to his own guilt, he was wrongly accusing her of betrayal. At that point he would have calmed down sufficiently to investigate the situation and find the truth. But then of course you would no longer have Shakespeare's *Othello*.

In terms of our own process, we do not have to get in touch with our horrendous guilt over betraying love in that original moment. First of all, there is no original moment; therefore any shadowy fragment of that illusory moment will do. Work with anything that causes you to get angry and upset right here and now. Stop and remind yourself that you are projecting. If you can *totally* forgive what is going on in the present, you will have forgiven everyone and everything. As *A Course in Miracles* says: "…thousands stand behind [your brother], and beyond each one of them there are a thousand more" (T-27.V.10:4); and behind each of those is God. The intensity we feel in certain situations when our buttons get pushed is the same as if we had gotten in touch with the guilt over killing off love. We all have been astonished by the intensity of our anger over something that should never have triggered such a reaction. For instance, perhaps someone I was expecting to call did not. That was all; yet I responded with absolute rage. The intensity comes, not from the specific situation, but from the general guilt. It does not matter whether it is something trivial or monumental—the guilt is the same.

Returning to the paragraph we have been discussing from "The Ego's Use of Guilt," what will help you get in touch with your ego is to recognize that anytime you are not peaceful—angry, upset, enraged, mildly annoyed, anxious, fearful, guilty, depressed—that is a red flag that says you are projecting something. Lesson 5 states "I am never upset for the reason I think." Being upset in any way should get your attention. The world of your special relationships can help you refocus, so that you return to the decision you made in your mind. This paragraph has explained the process: You identify with the ego, and from that point on you will feel you have attacked God, love, and truth. The enormity of the guilt over your seeming sin causes you to project it, and then inevitably fear you are going to be attacked in return.

Skip to paragraph 5, sentence 6. We will just read one sentence, which explains Othello's actions and our own:

(T-5.V.5:6) The ego believes that by punishing itself it will mitigate the punishment of God.

The context of this sentence is sickness, but the principle can easily be generalized. It helps us understand why we make mistakes when we know we are capable of not making them; why we sabotage our relationships, bodies, families, work, and so on. Behind all self-defeating behavior is the thought: "If *I* do the punishing, God will not. Therefore I will gladly suffer, for at least there is an *I* who suffers. If God punishes me, my self is extinguished." This one line from the text is simple, but it covers everything.

We turn now to a paragraph in "The Unbelievable Belief" in Chapter 7 of the text:

(T-7.VIII.3:8) The belief that by seeing it [guilt] outside you have excluded it from within is a complete distortion of the power of extension.

That is because *ideas leave not their source*. We believe ideas *do* leave their source, because that is how we came to exist as bodies and how the world was made. We believe by projecting guilt we are rid of it. But *ideas leave not their source*, which is why Jesus says there is no world out there (W-pI.132.6:2-3), and why he says that God did not create it. He teaches us that the world was made as an attack on God because it came from the original thought of attack (W-pII.3.2:1). We do not get rid of the guilt; we bury it. Yet through projection we have the magical illusion that guilt is in others, which justifies our thoughts of judgment, criticism, and hate, and the desire to kill them.

Othello did not have to deal with his guilt over betraying love because now he saw it clearly in his wife. Iago became his foil, just as Iago used others as foils to achieve his goal. This explains, once again, why Othello jumped on Iago's bandwagon as quickly as he did, and why he did not take the sensible steps that a normal person would have taken—to investigate for himself whether what Iago said was true. He did not because he did not *want* to know the truth. He needed to find someone he could accuse of betraying love. Who better than his pure and innocent wife?

(3:9-11) That is why those who project are vigilant for their own safety. They are afraid that their projections will return and hurt them. Believing they have blotted their projections from their own minds, they also believe their projections are trying to creep back in.

The guilt I attempt to get rid of is my own: I am the murderer and betrayer; the one who turned away from love and attacked it unfairly; the one who selfishly projected my guilt onto you. If you now have it, I perceive you as the betrayer; the one who attacked love out of self-ishness; and who cares only about how your needs are met. Such perception must be the truth because I literally made you in my image, just as we all did with God in the beginning. When God did not grant us special favor, we made of Him an unloving Father—*because we were an unloving Son.*

Again, this does not justify people's ego reactions, nor their cruelty and viciousness. The point is simply that when we let the behavior of others disturb our peace of mind that is a signal we are projecting. We are not responsible for the egos of others, but are responsible for our reactions to their egos. If we give them the power to take away our peace and the experience of God's Love, we are doing exactly what is described in this passage: Accusing ourselves of having taken away the peace of God by destroying love, we accuse ourselves of treating God unfairly and therefore everyone else. Guilt over our sin is what we project, and then perceive in everyone else.

Let me read those first two sentences again: "That is why those who project are vigilant for their own safety. They are afraid that their projections will return and hurt them." I see the projection of my sin, guilt, and hate outside me in others. Recall this startling passage in Lesson 134:

> When you feel that you are tempted to accuse someone of sin in
> any form, do not allow your mind to dwell on what you think he

did, for that is self-deception. Ask instead, "Would I accuse myself of doing this?" (W-pI.134.9:2-3).

It would have certainly ruined the play, but if Othello had read that lesson and done what it says, he would have stopped when he was accusing Desdemona and asked himself, "Would I accuse myself of doing
this?" Even if he were not in touch with the original thought of betraying love, he would have at least realized that his rage was unjustified.
That would have allowed him to proceed right-mindedly.

To reiterate this important point, *A Course in Miracles* does not tell
us we should not act in the world. It simply tells us not to act out of
hate or judgment, following the ego's dictates. "Do everything with
me," Jesus implores us. If Othello had followed the Course's teachings
he would have gone within and asked Jesus for help. He then would
have dealt with the situation more rationally, and things no doubt
would have turned out differently. However, Othello's guilt would not
allow that. He was compelled to protect his guilt, which is what this
next sentence describes:

**(3:12) Since the projections have not left their minds, they are
forced to engage in constant activity in order not to recognize this.**

That "constant activity" is everything we do to distract ourselves;
i.e., our special relationships—with ourselves, others, and everything
in the world. We engage in this constant activity so that we never have
to go within and look honestly at the guilt in our minds. We all hope
we can magically remove our guilt through projection, seeing others as
the evildoers. We then pursue them, whether as heads of state, heads
of a company, or heads of a family. Rather than project, however, we
could simply look within our minds. But if we are terrified of our guilt,
we must engage in "constant activity" to avoid such looking. Despite
our best attempts to believe in the magic of projection, we secretly
know that *the idea of guilt has never left its source in the mind*, and so
it is "forced to engage in constant activity in order not to recognize
this."

We have always to protect the guilt in our minds because the ego
tells us guilt is good. If you are without guilt, you are sinning against
the ego, as Jesus explains in the text: "To the ego, *the guiltless are
guilty*" (T-13.II.4:2). That means *the guilty are innocent*. In the ego system guilt is valued, and that is why we are attracted to it. Remember,

the first obstacle to peace is the *attraction* of guilt (T-19.IV-A.i). To the ego, guilt is good because guilt says we sinned. If we sinned, we have separated; and our separation makes us right and God wrong. Othello had to make Desdemona guilty because of his own guilt, seeing her as an unfaithful sinner and betrayer. He is a good example because he was not unfaithful to her as a husband, but he was unfaithful to what she represented—the Love of God. He acted out this betrayal by stealing her from her father, echoing what we all believe we have done: stolen love from our Father in Heaven.

One of the purposes of the workbook for students is help us spend time each day identifying how this dynamic of projection plays out in our personal lives. Jesus wants us to see how we continually seek to prove that he, God, and *A Course in Miracles* are wrong. Only then can we come to admit that we would prefer to be happy than right (T-29.VII.1:9). The next and concluding chapter helps us understand how Jesus helps us reach that happy goal.

Chapter 4

JESUS: TEACHING WITH GENTLE MEANS
AND EASY TASKS

We take our leave of the ego thought system as we continue with the same section we have been reading, "The Treachery of Specialness" (T-24.II). We learned that when we choose the specialness of separation we lose our awareness of the Love of God and can no longer hear His Voice. When our pain becomes great enough—not the pain of our most recent losses, which we reenact over and over again, but the pain of living a life governed by specialness—we throw up our hands in despair and say there must be another way, another teacher, another way of looking at things in this world. At that point meaningful change occurs, for we have allowed Jesus to come into the classroom of our lives and be our teacher, helping us learn a different way of perceiving everyone and everything.

Desdemona makes a wonderful statement that has nothing to do with the play itself, but brings to mind Jesus' loving and gentle means to support us as we learn from him. Although she is somewhat naive in not recognizing what is happening to her husband, she is caring and kind, with apparently no animosity towards anyone. She thus can say:

> *Those that do teach young babes*
> *Do it with gentle means and easy tasks....*

(IV,ii,111)

That is how Jesus teaches us: "*with gentle means and easy tasks.*" If there is something we cannot do—a person we are not ready to forgive, for example—he does not push us forward, demanding we be more spiritual. He does not throw *A Course in Miracles* in our face, as some of his students are wont to do. Rather, he waits patiently for our fear to abate; and his patience is infinite, as he reminds us:

I have shown you infinite patience because my will is that of our Father, from Whom I learned of infinite patience. His Voice was in me as It is in you, speaking for patience towards the Sonship in the Name of its Creator....Now you must learn that only infinite patience...calls upon infinite love... (T-5.VI.11:6-7; 12:1,3).

71

So, too, the Holy Spirit, our Teacher:

> One Teacher is in all minds and He teaches the same lesson to all. He always teaches you the inestimable worth of every Son of God, teaching it with infinite patience born of the infinite Love for which He speaks (T-7.VII.7:2-3).

Using our special relationships as the curriculum, Jesus teaches us his lessons of forgiveness. With his infinite patience—since he knows the outcome is sure—he gently reminds us how easy is our task, for all we need do is look with him at our ego's choices for specialness—not to change, resist, or fight against them. Like the Holy Spirit, whose manifestation he is, Jesus does not command us, nor demand we be less fearful than we are. He simply reminds us of our wrong choice, so we can make the correct one:

> The Voice of the Holy Spirit does not command, because It is incapable of arrogance. It does not demand, because It does not seek control. It does not overcome, because It does not attack. It merely reminds. It is compelling only because of what It reminds you *of*. It brings to your mind the other way, remaining quiet even in the midst of the turmoil you may make. The Voice for God is always quiet, because It speaks of peace (T-5.II.7:1-7).

Stated another way, guilt cannot be undone through manipulation of outer effects, but only through changing its cause—the mind's decision to listen to the wrong voice. Facilitating that change is Jesus' purpose as our teacher, and therefore it is the central focus of *A Course in Miracles*.

We turn now to paragraph 7 of "The Treachery of Specialness." In effect, this is what Jesus would say to us when we come to him sincerely seeking a better way, not merely asking for specific help with a specific problem, such as asking him to change the other person or some situation in the world, or how best to plot justified vengeance. Rather, we ask for help in perceiving the situations and conditions in our lives differently, realizing that the way we have been looking at them has not made us happy:

(T-24.II.7:1) You who have chained your savior to your specialness, and given it his place, remember this: He has not lost the power to forgive you all the sins you think you placed between him and the function of salvation given him for you.

Whoever your special love or hate partner is at the moment, that person is your savior, offering you an opportunity to redirect your attention from the outside relationship to the mind's relationship with the ego. We come to understand that the world is an "outside picture of an inward condition" (T-21.in.1:5), representing the inner wish to be separate and to blame someone else for it.

This shift has nothing to do with the other person *doing* anything for you. *A Course in Miracles* is never about *doing* anything. Instead, this sentence means that when I realize I have projected onto you and that you are not the problem, I recall the projections; I reverse what the ego has taught me, which was to go from inside to outside. Now I bring what was outside back within, realizing the guilt is not in you but in me. That is the meaning of my brother becoming my savior.

(7:2-3) Nor will you change his function, any more than you can change the truth in him and in yourself. But be you certain that the truth is just the same in both.

That last sentence is the key! All we ever need learn is this final message: "The truth is just the same in both." Specialness says the truth is in me, and what is in you is a lie; you say that the truth is in you, and the lie is in me. To the ego it is always *one or the other.* Recall that specialness is based upon differences. The undoing of that false perception—Jesus' answer to our specific requests—is to have us realize that everyone and every situation is the same. Not only is the truth the same in both of us; so is the illusion: We share the same Holy Spirit—His forgiveness—because we share the same wrong-minded hatred that the right mind corrects or undoes. Once again, this *is* Jesus' message: not to see anyone as different from ourselves. We are different in *form*, not *content.* Once again, since we share the same split mind we share the same ego, Holy Spirit, and decision maker that chooses between those two teachers.

(7:4-5) It [truth] gives no different messages and has one meaning. And it is one you and your brother both can understand, and one that brings release to both of you.

This is the key to our learning, and it is very simple: The ego does not recognize the words *same* and *both*—it knows only differences and *one or the other*—unlike the Holy Spirit, Who knows us all as the same—"together, or not at all" (T-19.IV-D.12:8).

(7:6) Here stands your brother with the key to Heaven in his hand, held out to you.

Why? Because he is your brother and is one with you. This has nothing to do with what he does or does not do, or even whether the person is physically alive. The person may even be someone you do not know but just heard about on the news or saw in a movie. We are dealing only with our projections, which we utilized in an attempt to get rid of the guilt that we now see in the other person, and are afraid will creep back in. This, again, has nothing to do with the objects of our projections, but only with what we have made of them—our image and likeness.

Returning to Othello, he secretly believed himself to be the betrayer of love, and so he made an image of his wife in his own likeness. That image was not based upon Desdemona's nature, for it consisted solely of the projections of Othello's guilt. Likewise, our anger at others has no basis in them, no matter what they may or may not have done. Their behavior notwithstanding, they do not have the power to take the peace of God away from us. And if not, what else could possibly matter to us? What else besides the peace of God is important? If, however, this peace does not matter to us, *that* then is the problem, which we need to look at. Clearly, then, we are valuing something other than God, as we all did at the beginning and continue to do in our special relationships.

(7:7-8) Let not the dream of specialness remain between you. What is one is joined in truth.

We are also joined as one in the illusion, for the ego thought system is one as well. We literally were cut from the same cloth of split-mindedness, half of which is the ego's thought system of separation and half of which is the Holy Spirit's thought system of Atonement. This thought is nicely echoed in the following passage from *The Gifts of God*, the prose poem Helen took down as a series of personal messages to her:

> But be sure of this and do not let it slip away: What God has joined is one. And one as well is everything that fear has made to be the great deceiver and the substitute for God's creation. You can choose but one, and which you choose is total (*The Gifts of God*, p. 117).

(8:1-2) Think of the loveliness that you will see within yourself, when you have looked on him as on a friend. He *is* the enemy of specialness, but only friend to what is real in you.

Once you make specialness your God and your identity, the world is a battleground and everyone your enemy, as it was with the ego's image of God the instant the Son took the tiny, mad idea seriously.

(8:3-7) Not one attack you thought you made on him has taken from him the gift that God would have him give to you. His need to give it is as great as yours to have it. Let him forgive you all your specialness, and make you whole in mind and one with him. He waits for your forgiveness only that he may return it unto you. It is not God Who has condemned His Son, but you, to save his specialness and kill his Self.

This is another explicit statement about what we believe we did: selfishly seeking to save our specialness, thereby having to kill our Self, Christ, which also meant killing His Father. We killed God and crucified His Son so our specialness would live. Once again, Jesus is not talking about anything specific or external, such as behavior or relationships—forgiveness occurs only in the mind, as does separation. If I forgive you, I will believe you have forgiven me. If I have not forgiven you, I will never believe you will forgive me, as we have already seen: "If he speaks not of Christ to you, you spoke not of Christ to him" (T-11.V.18:6).

Skip to the end of the section; paragraph 14.

(14:1-2) The key you threw away God gave your brother, whose holy hands would offer it to you when you were ready to accept His plan for your salvation in the place of yours. How could this readiness be reached save through the sight of all your misery, and the awareness that your plan has failed, and will forever fail to bring you peace and joy of any kind?

In the first sentence Jesus is saying we buried our guilt over throwing away the key to the Kingdom of Heaven, and, because we are all the same, then projected out what we had buried, placing it in someone else. When we realize that other people are not responsible for our lack of peace, we let them off the hook and correspondingly let ourselves off the hook as well. The ultimate realization is that there was no loss of

75

peace at all. Nothing happened. It is only when we believe that separation is a fact that we have the need to get rid of guilt by projecting it onto someone else.

The second sentence is equally significant. The only way we can attain the readiness to accept forgiveness and salvation is by our first recognizing how miserable we are. Our plan of specialness, hate, attack, and judgment was a colossal failure and led only to misery. Jesus tells us at the beginning of "The Happy Learner" in the text:

> The Holy Spirit needs a happy learner, in whom His mission can be happily accomplished. You who are steadfastly devoted to misery must first recognize that you are miserable and not happy. The Holy Spirit cannot teach without this contrast, for you believe misery *is* happiness (T-14.II.1:1-3).

Only by being aware of our misery can the Holy Spirit help us, and that is what Jesus is telling us here. We need to see that our plan has failed and that we are miserable as a result. We need to see what we are giving up. As we find ourselves about to commit the ego's sin of separation and attack once again, we must, unlike Othello, quickly become aware of the cost of what we are about to do, and decide we no longer want to pay the price. We must realize that killing off someone else because of his or her sin is not going to relieve us of our own. If anything, our attack will reinforce the belief in sin and guilt. In Othello's case, he reinforced his own sense of sin to such an extent that he had no recourse except to kill himself. His guilt was astronomical—completely intolerable and able to end only by his sacrifice at his own hand.

A Course in Miracles is not for people who think they are happy and their lives work; if so, there will be no motivation to change. To repeat this crucial thought: Jesus wants us to be aware of our misery, how our plan has failed and will forever fail to bring us lasting peace and joy. There has to be a part of us that must truly believe and sincerely want that happiness. To say the words "I want peace and joy" is nothing; but to really mean them is everything, as Jesus states in Lesson 185 (W-pI.185.1:2). We all would readily say: Yes, we want peace and joy. But we must realize that the peace and joy *A Course in Miracles* offers are radically different from what we ordinarily think, having nothing to do with anything external. They are purely internal states, for peace and joy come only from knowing that the Love of God is with us always: in our minds—not in anything external—and nothing can take It away from us. That awareness is the source of real joy.

(14:3) Through this despair you travel now, yet it is but illusion of despair.

Earlier in the text Jesus says that the Holy Spirit will walk with us through the circle of fear, through seeming terror, but God is on the other side (T-18.IX.3). It is *seeming* terror, and the world *seems* to be a world of despair for they are illusory. Nothing has changed. The Love of God is still what It is and has always been: "Not one note in Heaven's song was missed" (T-26.V.5:4).

(14:4-5) The death of specialness is not your death, but your awaking into life eternal. You but emerge from an illusion of what you are to the acceptance of yourself as God created you.

At the beginning of our dream of terror the ego told us that specialness was our life and the death of specialness would be our death. *A Course in Miracles* helps us step back from our identification with specialness so that we can begin to see that there is second self in us with which we could identify. Before we know we are the Self of Christ, we first must realize there is a self that is forgiving and not angry, despairing, depressed, or anxious; a happier, more peaceful, caring, and kind self. Step by step we begin to substitute the Holy Spirit's right-minded self of kindness, caring, and happiness for the ego's self of hatred, selfishness, and misery. At the very end of our journey both selves disappear, and all that remains is the Self we truly are as God created us.

And yet, as we have seen in our discussion of *Othello*, our attraction to the illusion of specialness, born of guilt, is the ego's primary defense against love. I will therefore close this chapter on Jesus with two of Helen's poems—"Bright Stranger" and "The Second Chance"—that illustrate the ego's unsuccessful attempts to kill love—his love—and depict our perceived betrayal and defenses that seek to protect our self from love's truth. The first of these is more general in its presentation of the need to keep our love away with "locks and keys." Yet all our attempts fail in the end before "the gentleness with which he looked at me." Jesus' kind and loving presence serves as the reminder that allows His holy Name to once more flood our awareness, remind us that His Name is ours, and that the bright stranger, in the end, is our Self.

Bright Stranger

Strange was my Love to me. For when He came
I did not know Him. And He seemed to me
To be but an intruder on my peace.
I did not see the gifts He brought, nor hear
His soft appeal. I tried to shut Him out
With locks and keys that merely fell away
Before His coming. I could not escape
The gentleness with which He looked at me.
I asked Him in unwillingly, and turned
Away from Him. But He held out His hand
And asked me to remember Him. In me
An ancient Name began to stir and break
Across my mind in gold. The light embraced
Me deep in silence till He spoke the Word,
And then at last I recognized my Lord.

(The Gifts of God, p. 43)

This next poem is even more explicit about our seeming betrayal and use of hate as a defense. Yet the gentle and forgiving eyes of Jesus meet ours of fear and guilt, and their hate dissolve as his voice touches our heart. Our hate brought to his love can no longer stand, and in its place is seen the star of Christ—the sign of Christ's rebirth in us—shining brightly within our minds (T-15.XI.2:1-2). Unlike poor Othello, we have a second chance, which patiently awaits our choosing it:

The Second Chance

I have betrayed my God in many ways,
Throughout the bitter nights and secret days.
My hate drove deep into my mind, and tore
Away the little love I had in store.
I watched it go without regret, for I
Did not perceive how much I lost thereby.
With hatred as a friend, I did not fear
To lose it for a god I held more dear.
For now I seemed secure, by hate held fast,
And feeling I was safe from love at last.

> The eyes of Christ looked steadily on me
> As if my secret hate He did not see.
> I hugged it tight and hid it in my heart,
> And still I held if from His Love apart.
> Until one day my eyes met His, and then
> My fingers opened and my heart. And when
> I looked away a star was in my hand;
> Another in my heart. I listened, and
> His voice said silently to me, "Now go
> And hate no more." And I said, "Be it so."
> *(The Gifts of God,* p. 45)

Thus we have Jesus' sixth act, the forgiving resolution of our five-act drama of sin, guilt, and hate-filled vengeance. Jesus' gentle and comforting presence is the reminder how easy is our task of letting go of what we never truly wanted, and which never truly existed as a barrier to the truth of Who we are as God's one Son.

79

CLOSING MEDITATION

CHOOSE ONCE AGAIN

I close by reading three paragraphs from the end of the text as a meditation, without commentary. They are a beautiful and helpful summary of everything we have discussed. Their main thrust is choosing again. In fact, the text ends with the section called "Choose Once Again," and we can say that this is the right-minded message of not only *Othello*, but the other tragedies we have been discussing. All four tragic heroes chose to listen to the wrong voice, and we have just examined how, because of his guilt, Othello chose to listen to that voice. However, as students of *A Course in Miracles* we are becoming increasingly aware of our self-hatred, and that we can ask for help to undo it at any time. Thus, everything in the Course comes down to these final paragraphs about choosing again. This entails becoming aware of what it is we are choosing *against*, so that our choosing *for* love will be more meaningful. The darkness of guilt and hate, looked at with forgiveness, always gives way to love's bright and kindly light. And so we give the radiant love of Jesus' wisdom the final word, gently reminding us to choose again:

Be vigilant against temptation, then, remembering that it is but a wish, insane and meaningless, to make yourself a thing that you are not. And think as well upon the thing that you would be instead. It is a thing of madness, pain and death; a thing of treachery and black despair, of failing dreams and no remaining hope except to die, and end the dream of fear. *This* is temptation; nothing more than this. Can this be difficult to choose *against*? Consider what temptation is, and see the real alternatives you choose between. There are but two. Be not deceived by what appears as many choices. There is hell or Heaven, and of these you choose but one....

You *are* as God created you, and so is every living thing you look upon, regardless of the images you see. What you behold as sickness and as pain, as weakness and as suffering and loss, is but temptation to perceive yourself defenseless

81

and in hell. Yield not to this, and you will see all pain, in every form, wherever it occurs, but disappear as mists before the sun. A miracle has come to heal God's Son, and close the door upon his dreams of weakness, opening the way to his salvation and release. Choose once again what you would have him be, remembering that every choice you make establishes your own identity as you will see it and believe it is. . . .

Let us be glad that we can walk the world, and find so many chances to perceive another situation where God's gift can once again be recognized as ours! And thus will all the vestiges of hell, the secret sins and hidden hates be gone. And all the loveliness which they concealed appear like lawns of Heaven to our sight, to lift us high above the thorny roads we travelled on before the Christ appeared. Hear me, my brothers, hear and join with me. God has ordained I cannot call in vain, and in His certainty I rest content. For you *will* hear, and you *will* choose again. And in this choice is everyone made free (T-31.VII.14; VIII.6,9).

APPENDIX

Iago's Credo

I believe in a cruel God, who has created me
In his image and whom, in anger, I name.
From some vile germ or atom
Am I born.
I am wicked
Because I am human;
And I feel the primeval slime in me.

Yes! This is my creed!
I believe with a firm heart, as ever does
The widow praying at the temple,
That whatever evil I think or do
Was decreed for me by fate.

I believe that a just man is but an hysterical actor,
Both in face and heart,
That everything in him is a lie:
Tears, kisses, glances,
Sacrifices and honor.

And I believe man to be fortune's fool
From the germ of the cradle
To the worm of the grave.

And after all this mockery comes Death.
And then? And then? Death is nothingness.
And Heaven is an ancient lie.

(Arrigo Boito)

A Course in Miracles

The world you see is the delusional system of those made mad by guilt. Look carefully at this world, and you will realize that this is so. For this world is the symbol of punishment, and all the laws that seem to govern it are the laws of death. Children are born into it through pain and in pain. Their growth is attended by suffering, and they learn of sorrow and separation and death. Their minds seem to be trapped in their brain, and its powers to decline if their bodies are hurt. They seem to love, yet they desert and are deserted. They appear to lose what they love, perhaps the most insane belief of all. And their bodies wither and gasp and are laid in the ground, and are no more. Not one of them but has thought that God is cruel.

(T-13.in.2:2-10)

INDEX OF REFERENCES TO *A COURSE IN MIRACLES*

text

T-2.III.3:3	12	T-18.IX.3	77
T-3.V.6:3	61	T-18.IX.3-5	15
T-4.VII.5	6	T-19.IV-A.i	68
T-5.II.7	72	T-19.IV-D.12:8	73
T-5.V.3:1-2	63-64	T-20.IV.5:3	12
T-5.V.5:6	66	T-21.in.1	13
T-5.VI.11:6-7; 12:1,3	71	T-21.in.1:5	73
T-7.VII.7:2-3	72	T-22.III.6:7	57
T-7.VIII.3:8	66-68	T-23.II	15
T-10.I.2:1	11	T-23.II.2:1-3	57
T-11.IV.6	47	T-23.II.9	14
T-11.V.18:6	64, 75	T-23.II.13	14
T-13.in.2	14	T-23.IV.9:8	58
T-13.in.2:2	13	T-24	51
T-13.II.4:2	68	T-24.II	71
T-13.III.4;5:3-4	55-56	T-24.II.3:1	52-58
T-13-III.10:1	41-47	T-24.II.7:1	72-77
T-13.VII.9:7	45	T-24.III.8:13	44
T-13.IX	10	T-24.VII.10	13
T-14.II.1:1-3	76	T-26.I	49
T-15.V.8:3-5	45	T-26.V.5:4	77
T-15.XI.2:1-2	78	T-26.VIII.1:3-5	17
T-16.V	6	T-26.X.4:1	44, 48
T-16.V.4:1	47-48	T-27.V.10:4	65
T-16.V.10:1	47	T-27.VIII.6:2	3
T-16.V.12:1-5	54	T-28	16
T-17.IV	50	T-29	16
T-17.VI	8	T-29.VII.1:9	69
T-18.I.5:6-6:2	11	T-31.VII.14	81
T-18.VI.1:4-6	49	T-31.VIII.6	81-82
T-18.VIII.2:5-3:4	5	T-31.VIII.9	82
T-18.VIII.4:1	5		

workbook for students

W-pI.5 65-66

W-pI.93.1:1 15

W-pI.132 13

W-pI.132.6:2-3 66

W-pI.134.9:2-3 67-68

W-pI.151.7:2-3 58

W-pI.151.10:2 58

W-pI.151.11:3 58

W-pI.151.12:3-4 58

W-pI.185.1:2 76

W-pII.3.2:1 66

manual for teachers

M-1.1:1-2 46

M-17.7:3-4 15

M-25 59

The Song of Prayer

S-1.I.2:1-2 61

S-1.I.4:6-8 62

The Gifts of God

"Bright Stranger" (p. 43) 78

"Gifts of God" (p. 117) 74

"Second Chance" (p. 45) 78-79

Foundation for A Course in Miracles®

Kenneth Wapnick received his Ph.D. in Clinical Psychology in 1968 from Adelphi University. He was a close friend and associate of Helen Schucman and William Thetford, the two people whose joining together was the immediate stimulus for the scribing of A Course in Miracles. Kenneth has been involved with A Course in Miracles since 1973, writing, teaching, and integrating its principles with his practice of psychotherapy. He is on the Executive Board of the Foundation for Inner Peace, publishers of A Course in Miracles.

In 1983, with his wife Gloria, he began the Foundation for A Course in Miracles, and in 1984 this evolved into a Teaching and Healing Center in Crompond, New York, which was quickly outgrown. In 1988 they opened the Academy and Retreat Center in upstate New York. In 1995 they began the Institute for Teaching Inner Peace through A Course in Miracles, an educational corporation chartered by the New York State Board of Regents. In 2001 the Foundation moved to Temecula, California and shifted its emphasis to electronic teaching. The Foundation publishes a quarterly newsletter, "The Lighthouse," which is available free of charge. The following is Kenneth and Gloria's vision of the Foundation.

In our early years of studying *A Course in Miracles,* as well as teaching and applying its principles in our respective professions of psychotherapy, and teaching and school administration, it seemed evident that this was not the simplest of thought systems to understand. This was so not only in the intellectual grasp of its teachings, but perhaps more importantly in the application of these teachings to our personal lives. Thus, it appeared to us from the beginning that the Course lent itself to teaching, parallel to the ongoing teachings of the Holy Spirit in the daily opportunities within our relationships, which are discussed in the early pages of the manual for teachers.

One day several years ago while Helen Schucman and I (Kenneth) were discussing these ideas, she shared a vision that she had had of a teaching center as a white temple with a gold cross atop it. Although it was clear that this image was symbolic, we understood it to be representative of what the teaching center was to be: a place where the person of Jesus and his message in *A Course in Miracles* would be manifest. We have sometimes seen an image of a lighthouse shining its light into the sea, calling to it those passers-by who sought it. For us, this light is the Course's teaching of forgiveness, which we would hope to share with those who are drawn to the Foundation's form of teaching and its vision of *A Course in Miracles*.

This vision entails the belief that Jesus gave the Course at this particular time in this particular form for several reasons. These include:

1) the necessity of healing the mind of its belief that attack is salvation; this is accomplished through forgiveness, the undoing of our belief in the reality of separation and guilt.

2) emphasizing the importance of Jesus and/or the Holy Spirit as our loving and gentle Teacher, and developing a personal relationship with this Teacher.

3) correcting the errors of Christianity, particularly where it has emphasized suffering, sacrifice, separation, and sacrament as being inherent in God's plan for salvation.

Our thinking has always been inspired by Plato (and his mentor Socrates), both the man and his teachings. Plato's Academy was a place where serious and thoughtful people came to study his philosophy in an atmosphere conducive to their learning, and then returned to their professions to implement what they were taught by the great philosopher. Thus, by integrating abstract philosophical ideals with experience, Plato's school seemed to be the perfect model for the teaching center that we directed for so many years.

We therefore see the Foundation's principal purpose as being to help students of *A Course in Miracles* deepen their understanding of its thought system, conceptually and experientially, so that they may be more effective instruments of Jesus' teaching in their own lives. Since teaching forgiveness without experiencing it is empty, one of the Foundation's specific goals is to help facilitate the process whereby people may be better able to know that their own sins are forgiven and that they are truly loved by God. Thus is the Holy Spirit able to extend His Love through them to others.

Responding in part to the "electronic revolution," we have taken the Foundation's next step in our move to Temecula, California. With this move to a non-residential setting we are shifting our focus, though not exclusively, from totally live presentations to electronic and digital forms of teaching in order to maximize the benefits of the burgeoning field of electronic media communication. This will allow us to increase our teaching outreach, the *content* of which will remain the same, allowing its *form* to adapt to the 21st century.

RELATED MATERIAL ON *A COURSE IN MIRACLES*®

By Kenneth Wapnick, Ph.D.

Books

(For full descriptions please see our Web site at www.facim.org
or call or write for our free catalog)

CHRISTIAN PSYCHOLOGY IN *A COURSE IN MIRACLES.*® Second edition,
enlarged.
ISBN 0-933291-14-0 • #B-1• Paperback • 90 pages $5
Audio version of the second edition of the book,
read by Kenneth Wapnick • #T2 $10

Available also in Spanish:
PSICOLOGIA CRISTIANA EN *UN CURSO EN MILAGROS*®
ISBN 0-933291-17-5 • #B-1s • Paperback • 114 pages $5

A TALK GIVEN ON *A COURSE IN MIRACLES:*® An Introduction.
Seventh edition.
ISBN 0-933291-16-7 • #B-3 • Paperback • 131 pages $6

Available also in Spanish:
UNA INTRODUCCION BASICA A *UN CURSO EN MILAGROS*®
ISBN 0-933291-10-8 • #B-3s • Paperback • 159 pages $6

Available also in Portuguese:
UMA INTRODUÇÃO BÁSICA A *UM CURSO EM MILAGRES*®
ISBN 0-933291-27-2 • #B-3p • Paperback • 145 pages $5

*Available also in German:*1
EINFÜHRUNG IN *EIN KURS IN WUNDERN*®

Available also in Dutch:
INLEIDING TOT *A COURSE IN MIRACLES*®
Order from: Ankh-Hermes bv • Postbus 125 • 7400 AC Deventer • Netherlands

Available also in French:
INTRODUCTION GENERALE A *UN COURS SUR LES MIRACLES*®
ISBN 0-933291-26-4 • #B-3f • Paperback • 145 pages $6

Available also in Danish:
INTRODUKTION TIL *ET KURSES I MIRAKLER*®
Order from: SphinX Publishers • Løvstræde 8 • 1152 København K • Denmark

Available also in Italian:
INTRODUZIONE A *UN CORSO IN MIRACOLI*®
Order from: Gruppo Editoriale Armenia • Via Valtellina, 63 • 20129 Milano, Italy

---

1 *All German translations may be ordered from*:
Greuthof Verlag und Vertrieb GmbH • Herrenweg 2 • D 79261 Gutach i. Br. • Germany • Tel.
07681-6025 • FAX 07681-6027

GLOSSARY-INDEX FOR *A COURSE IN MIRACLES*.® Fifth edition, revised and enlarged.
ISBN 0-933291-03-5 • #B-4 • Softcover • 349 pages $10

Available also in Spanish:
GLOSARIO-INDICE PARA *UN CURSO EN MILAGROS*®
ISBN 0-933291-20-5 • #B-4s • Paperback • 245 pages $10

Available also in German:
GLOSSAR ZU *EIN KURS IN WUNDERN*®

FORGIVENESS AND JESUS: The Meeting Place of *A Course in Miracles*® and Christianity. Sixth edition.
ISBN 0-933291-13-2 • #B-5 • Paperback • 399 pages $16

Available also in Spanish:
EL PERDON Y JESUS: El punto de encuentro entre *Un curso en milagros*® y el cristianismo.
ISBN 0-933291-23-X • #B-5s • Paperback • 435 pages $16

Available also in German:
DIE VERGEBUNG UND JESUS

THE FIFTY MIRACLE PRINCIPLES OF *A COURSE IN MIRACLES*.® Fifth edition.
ISBN 0-933291-15-9 • #B-6 • Paperback • 107 pages $8

Available also in Spanish:
LOS CINCUENTA PRINCIPIOS DEL MILAGRO DE *UN CURSO EN MILAGROS*®
ISBN 0-933291-19-1 • #B-6s • Paperback • 139 pages $8

Available also in German:
WUNDER ALS WEG

AWAKEN FROM THE DREAM. Second Edition. Gloria and Kenneth Wapnick.
ISBN 0-933291-04-3 • #B-7 • Paperback • 132 pages $10

Available in German:
VON TRAUM ERWACHEN

THE OBSTACLES TO PEACE.
ISBN 0-933291-05-1 • #B-8 • Paperback • 295 pages $12

LOVE DOES NOT CONDEMN: The World, the Flesh, and the Devil According to Platonism, Christianity, Gnosticism, and *A Course in Miracles*.®
ISBN 0-933291-07-8 • #B-9 • Hardcover • 614 pages $25

A VAST ILLUSION: Time According to *A Course in Miracles*.® Second edition.
ISBN 0-933291-09-4 • #B-10 • Paperback • 345 pages $12

Available also in German:
DIE ILLUSION DER ZEIT

ABSENCE FROM FELICITY: The Story of Helen Schucman and Her Scribing of *A Course in Miracles.*® Second Edition.
ISBN 0-933291-08-6 • #B-11 • Paperback • 498 pages $17
Available also in German:
JENSEITS DER GLÜCKSELIGKEIT

OVEREATING: A Dialogue. An Application of the Principles of *A Course in Miracles.*® Second Edition.
ISBN 0-933291-11-6 • #B-12 • Paperback • 70 pages $5

A COURSE IN MIRACLES® AND CHRISTIANITY: A DIALOGUE.
Kenneth Wapnick and W. Norris Clarke, S.J.
ISBN 0-933291-18-3 • #B-13 • Paperback • 110 pages $7
Available also in Spanish:
UN CURSO DE MILAGROS® Y EL CRISTIANISMO: Un Dialogo
ISBN 0-933291-22-1 • #B-13s • Paperback • 117 pages $7
Available also in German:
EIN KURS IN WUNDERN® UND DAS CHRISTENTUM - EIN DIALOG

THE MOST COMMONLY ASKED QUESTIONS ABOUT *A COURSE IN MIRACLES.*® Gloria and Kenneth Wapnick.
ISBN 0-933291-21-3 • #B-14 • Paperback • 144 pages $8
Available also in Spanish:
LAS PREGUNTAS MAS COMUNES EN TORNO A *UN CURSO EN MILAGROS*®
ISBN 0-933291-28-0 • #B-14s • Paperback • 155 pages $8
Available also in German:
DER HIMMEL HAT KEIN GEGENTEIL
Available also in Dutch:
DE MEEST GESTELDA VRAGEN OVER *EEN CURSUS IN WONDEREN*®
Order from: Ankh-Hermes bv • Postbus 125 • 7400 AC Deventer • Netherlands

THE MESSAGE OF *A COURSE IN MIRACLES.*®
   Volume One, *All Are Called.*
   Volume Two, *Few Choose to Listen.*
Volume One 380 pages; Volume Two 239 pages
ISBN 0-933291-25-6 • #B-15 • Paperback $22 (two-volume set)
Available also in German:
DIE BOTSCHAFT VON *EIN KURS IN WUNDERN*®
Available also in Spanish:
EL MENSAJE DE *UN CURSO EN MILAGROS*®

THE JOURNEY HOME: "The Obstacles to Peace" in *A Course in Miracles.*®
ISBN 0-933291-24-8 • #B-16 • paperback • 510 pages $16.95

ENDING OUR RESISTANCE TO LOVE: The Practice of *A Course in Miracles.*®
ISBN 1-59142-132-2 • #B-17 • paperback • 94 pages $5

Video Tape Albums
(For full descriptions please see our Web site at www.facim.org or call or write for our free catalog)

SEEK NOT TO CHANGE THE COURSE. Reflections on *A Course in Miracles.*®
#V1 • 135 mins. • VHS $30 • PAL (non-U.S.) $40
See also #T16 in Audio Tape and CD section.

THE REAL WORLD (Three-hour unedited workshop). Gloria and Kenneth Wapnick.
ISBN 0-933291-99-X • #V3 • 3 hrs. • VHS (US) $30 • PAL (non-US) $40.

THE REAL WORLD (Two-hour edited workshop). Gloria and Kenneth Wapnick.
ISBN 0-933291-98-1 • #V4 • 2 hrs. • VHS (US) $20 • PAL (non-US) $30.

AN INTERVIEW WITH KENNETH AND GLORIA WAPNICK. A one-hour interview conducted by Corinne Edwards at the Miracle Network in Chicago in December 1995.
#V5 • 1 hr. • VHS (US) $15 • PAL (non US) $20.

VISIONARIES. This 18-minute video was produced for the PBS series, *Visionaries*, and is narrated by Sam Waterston.
#V6 • 18-min. • VHS (US) $10

THE PATHWAY OF FORGIVENESS.
ISBN 1-59142-008-3 • #V7 • 4 hr. • VHS (US) $30 • PAL (non-U.S.) $40
See also #T64 in Audio Tapes and CDs section.

LIVING *A COURSE IN MIRACLES*®
ISBN 1-59142-009-1 • #V8 • two 2-hr. tapes • VHS (US) $30 • PAL (non-U.S.) $40
See also #T67 in Audio Tapes and CDs section.

THE MEANING OF THE HOLY INSTANT.
ISBN 1-59142-010-5 • #V9 • 2-hr. • VHS $20 • PAL (non-U.S.) $3o
See also #T62 in Audio Tapes and CDs section.

SPECIAL RELATIONSHIPS: The Home Of Guilt.
ISBN 1-59142-012-1 • #V10 • two 2-hr. tapes • VHS $30 •
PAL (non-U.S.) $40
See also #T68 in Audio Tapes and CDs section.

LOVE AND BE SILENT: King Lear, Defenselessness, and *A Course in Miracles.*®
ISBN 1-59142-013-X • #V11 • two 2-hr. tapes • VHS $30 •
PAL (non-U.S.) $40
See also #T65 in Audio Tapes and CDs section.

CLASSES ON THE TEXT OF *A COURSE IN MIRACLES*®.
Introduction • ISBN 1-59142-022-9 • #V12-in • 1 tape • VHS (US) $15
Chapter 1 • ISBN 1-59142-023-7 • #V12-1 • 1 tape • VHS (US) $15
Chapter 2 • ISBN 1-59142-024-5 • #V12-2 • 1 tape • VHS (US) $15
Chapter 3 • ISBN 1-59142-025-3 • #V12-3 • 1 tape • VHS (US) $15
Chapter 4 • ISBN 1-59142-026-1 • #V12-4 • 1 tape • VHS (US) $15
Chapter 5 • ISBN 1-59142-027-X • #V12-5 • 1 tape • VHS (US) $15
Chapter 6 • ISBN 1-59142-028-8 • #V12-6 • 1 tape • VHS (US) $15
Chapter 7 • ISBN 1-59142-029-6 • #V12-7 • 1 tape • VHS (US) $15
Chapter 8 • ISBN 1-59142-030-X • #V12-8 • 1 tape • VHS (US) $15
Chapter 9 • ISBN 1-59142-031-8 • #V12-9 • 1 tape • VHS (US) $15
Chapter 10 • ISBN 1-59142-032-6 • #V12-10 • 1 tape • VHS (US) $15
Chapter 11 • ISBN 1-59142-033-4 • #V12-11 • 1 tape • VHS (US) $15
Chapter 12 • ISBN 1-59142-034-2 • #V12-12 • 1 tape • VHS (US) $15
Chapter 13 • ISBN 1-59142-035-0 • #V12-13 • 1 tape • VHS (US) $15
Chapter 14 • ISBN 1-59142-036-9 • #V12-14 • 1 tape • VHS (US) $15
Chapter 15 • ISBN 1-59142-037-7 • #V12-15 • 1 tape • VHS (US) $15
Chapter 16 • ISBN 1-59142-038-5 • #V12-16 • 1 tape • VHS (US) $15
Chapter 17 • ISBN 1-59142-039-3 • #V12-17 • 1 tape • VHS (US) $15
Chapter 18 • ISBN 1-59142-040-7 • #V12-18 • 1 tape • VHS (US) $15
Chapter 19 • ISBN 1-59142-041-5 • #V12-19 • 1 tape • VHS (US) $15
Chapter 20 • ISBN 1-59142-042-3 • #V12-20 • 1 tape • VHS (US) $15
Chapter 21 • ISBN 1-59142-043-1 • #V12-21 • 1 tape • VHS (US) $15
Chapter 22 • ISBN 1-59142-044-X • #V12-22 • 1 tape • VHS (US) $15
Chapter 23 • ISBN 1-59142-045-8 • #V12-23 • 1 tape • VHS (US) $15
Chapter 24 • ISBN 1-59142-046-6 • #V12-24 • 1 tape • VHS (US) $15
Chapter 25 • ISBN 1-59142-047-4 • #V12-25 • 1 tape • VHS (US) $15
Chapter 26 • ISBN 1-59142-048-2 • #V12-26 • 1 tape • VHS (US) $15
Chapter 27 • ISBN 1-59142-049-0 • #V12-27 • 1 tape • VHS (US) $15
Chapter 28 • ISBN 1-59142-050-4 • #V12-28 • 1 tape • VHS (US) $15
Chapter 29 • ISBN 1-59142-051-2 • #V12-29 • 1 tape • VHS (US) $15
Chapter 30 • ISBN 1-59142-052-0 • #V12-30 • 1 tape • VHS (US) $15
Chapter 31 • ISBN 1-59142-053-9 • #V12-31 • 1 tape • VHS (US) $15
See also #T61-1 through T61-8 in Audio Tapes and CDs section.
See also #CD61-1 through CD61-8 in Audio Tapes and CDs section.

JUSTICE RETURNED TO LOVE.
ISBN 1-59142-054-7 • #V13 • two 2-hr. tapes • VHS (US) $30
See also #T81 in Audio Tapes and CDs section.

THE TIME MACHINE.
ISBN 1-59142-055-5 • #V14 • two 2-hr. tapes • VHS (US) $30
See also #T73 in Audio Tapes and CDs section.

FORGIVENESS AND THE END OF TIME.
ISBN 1-59142-067-9 • #V15 • two 2-hr. tapes • VHS (US) $30
See also #T74 in Audio Tapes and CDs section.

FROM DARKNESS TO LIGHT.
ISBN 1-59142-068-7 • #V16 • two 2-hr. tapes • VHS (US) $30
See also #T63 in Audio Tapes and CDs section.

JESUS: Symbol and Reality.
ISBN 1-59142-069-5 • #V17 • two 2-hr. tapes • VHS (US) $30
See also #T66 in Audio Tapes and CDs section.

DREAMING THE DREAM.
ISBN 1-59142-070-9 • #V18 • two 2-hr. tapes • VHS (US) $30
See also #T69 in Audio Tapes and CDs section.

THE COMPASSION OF THE MIRACLE.
ISBN 1-59142-071-7 • #V19 • two 2-hr. tapes • VHS (US) $30
See also #T70 in Audio Tapes and CDs section.

HEALING THE DREAM OF SICKNESS.
ISBN 1-59142-072-5 • #V20 • two 2-hr. tapes • VHS (US) $30
See also #T75 in Audio Tapes and CDs section.

THE CHANGELESS DWELLING PLACE.
ISBN 1-59142-077-6 • #V21 • two 2-hr. tapes • VHS (US) $30
See also #T76 in Audio Tapes and CDs section.

TO BE OR NOT TO BE: Hamlet, Death, and *A Course in Miracles.*®
ISBN 1-59142-079-2 • #V22 • two 2-hr. tapes • VHS (US) $30
See also #T77 in Audio Tapes and CDs section.

FORM VS. CONTENT: Sex and Money.
ISBN 1-59142-080-6 • #V23 • two 2-hr. tapes • VHS (US) $30
See also #T78 in Audio Tapes and CDs section.

THE PRODIGAL SON.
ISBN 1-59142-081-4 • #V24 • two 2-hr. tapes • VHS (US) $30
See also #T79 in Audio Tapes and CDs section.

THE PROBLEM OF EVIL.
ISBN 1-59142-095-4 • #V25 • two 2-hr. tapes • VHS (US) $30
See also #T82 in Audio Tapes and CDs section.

CLASSES ON THE MANUAL FOR TEACHERS OF *A COURSE IN MIRACLES.*®
Volume 1 • Introduction; Sections 1–3 • ISBN 1-59142-085-7 • #V26-1 • 1 tape • VHS (US)$15
Volume 2 • Section 4 • ISBN 1-59142-086-5 • #V26-2 • 1 tape • VHS (US)$15
Volume 3 • Sections 5–8 • ISBN 1-59142-087-3 • #V26-3 • 1 tape • VHS (US)$15
Volume 4 • Sections 9–13 • ISBN 1-59142-088-1 • #V26-4 • 1 tape • VHS (US)$15
Volume 5 • Sections 14–17 • ISBN 1-59142-089-X • #V26-5 • 1 tape • VHS (US)$15
Volume 6 • Sections 18–21 • ISBN 1-59142-090-3 • #V26-6 • 1 tape • VHS (US)$15
Volume 7 • Sections 22–25 • ISBN 1-59142-091-1 • #V26-7 • 1 tape • VHS (US)$15
Volume 8 • Sections 26–29 • ISBN 1-59142-0092-X • #V26-8 • 1 tape • VHS (US)$15
Volume 9 • Clarification of Terms, Part 1 • ISBN 1-59142-093-8 • #V26-9 • 1 tape • VHS (US)$15
Volume 10 • Clarification of Terms, Part 2 • ISBN 1-59142-094-6 • #V26-10 • 1 tape • VHS (US)$15
See also #T83-1 and T83-2 in Audio Tapes and CDs section.
See also #CD83-1 and CD83-2 in Audio Tapes and CDs section.

THE QUALITY OF MERCY.
ISBN 1-59142-099-7 • #V27 • two 2-hr. tapes • VHS (US) $30
See also #T84 in Audio Tapes and CDs section.

A TALE TOLD BY AN IDIOT: Macbeth, Guilt, and *A Course in Miracles.*®
ISBN 1-59142-102-0 • #V28 • two 2-hr. tapes • VHS (US) $30
See also #T85 in Audio Tapes and CDs section.

HEALING: Hearing the Melody
ISBN 1-59142-112-8 • #V29 • two 2-hr. tapes • VHS (US) $30
See also #T88 and #CD88 in the Audio Tapes and CDs section.

LOVING NOT WISELY BUT TOO WELL: Othello, Specialness and *A Course in Miracles.*®
ISBN 1-59142-131-4 • #V30 • two 2-hr. tapes • VHS (US) $30
See also #T90 and #CD90 in the Audio Tapes and CDs section.

AN INTRODUCTION TO *A COURSE IN MIRACLES*®
ISBN 1-59142-133-0 • #V31 • one 98 min. tape • VHS (US) $10

Audio Tapes and Compact Discs
Classes and Workshops
*(For full descriptions please see our Web site at www.facim.org
or call or write for our free catalog)*

CHRISTIAN PSYCHOLOGY IN *A COURSE IN MIRACLES.*® Audio version of the
second edition of the book, read by Kenneth Wapnick.
Tapes: ISBN 0-933291-50-7 • #T2 • 2 tapes $10

THE SIMPLICITY OF SALVATION.
Tapes: ISBN 0-933291-51-5 • #T1 • 8 tapes $48

ATONEMENT WITHOUT SACRIFICE: Christianity, the Bible, and the Course.
Tapes: ISBN 0-933291-53-1 • #T3 • 2 tapes $10

THE EGO AND FORGIVENESS. Introductory overview of the Course.
Tapes: ISBN 0-933291-55-8 • #T5 • 2 tapes $10
Available also in German:
DAS EGO UND DIE VERGEBUNG

SPECIAL RELATIONSHIPS—PART 1.
Tapes: ISBN 0-933291-59-0 • #T9 • 8 tapes $48

SPECIAL RELATIONSHIPS—PART 2.
Tapes: ISBN 0-933291-60-4 • #T10 • 6 tapes $36

CAUSE AND EFFECT.
Tapes: ISBN 0-933291-63-9 • #T13 • 8 tapes $48

THE GIFTS OF GOD. A discussion of the inspired poetry of Helen Schucman.
Tapes: ISBN 0-933291-65-5 • #T15 • 3 tapes $18
CDs: ISBN 1-59142-141-1 • #CD15 • 4 CDs $25

SEEK NOT TO CHANGE THE COURSE: Reflections on *A Course in Miracles.*®
Gloria and Kenneth Wapnick. Audio version of video tape of the same name.
Tapes: ISBN 0-933291-66-3 • #T16 • 2 tapes $10

LOVE DOES NOT OPPOSE. Gloria and Kenneth Wapnick.
Tapes: ISBN 0-933291-67-1 • #T17 • 8 tapes $48

THE SONG OF PRAYER.
Tapes: ISBN 0-933291-68-X • #T18 • 10 tapes $60
CDs: ISBN 1-59142-136-5 • #CD18 • 13 CDs $70

THE ORIGIN OF *A COURSE IN MIRACLES.*®
Tapes: ISBN 0-933291-69-8 • #T19 • 1 tape $6

I WILL BE STILL AN INSTANT AND GO HOME.
Tapes: ISBN 0-933291-70-1 • #T20 • 1 tape $6

JESUS: Teacher of Forgiveness • Model of Resurrection.
Tapes: ISBN 0-933291-71-X • #T21 • 8 tapes $48

THE AUTHORITY PROBLEM.
Tapes: ISBN 0-933291-72-8 • #T22 • 5 tapes $30

OUR GRATITUDE TO GOD.
Tapes: ISBN 0-933291-73-6 • #T23 • 5 tapes $30

SICKNESS AND HEALING.
Tapes: ISBN 0-933291-74-4 • #T24 • 8 tapes $48

WHAT IT MEANS TO BE A TEACHER OF GOD.
Tapes: ISBN 0-933291-75-2 • #T25 • 6 tapes $36

OVEREATING: A Dialogue. An Application of the Principles of *A Course in Miracles.*®
Tapes: ISBN 0-933291-76-0 • #T26 • 1 tape $6

TO JUDGE OR NOT TO JUDGE.
Tapes: ISBN 0-933291-77-9 • #T27 • 4 tapes $24

HEALING THE UNHEALED HEALER.
Tapes: ISBN 0-933291-78-7 • #T28 • 8 tapes $48

THE REAL WORLD: Our Home away from Home.
Tapes: ISBN 0-933291-79-5 • #T29 • 8 tapes $48

TRUE EMPATHY: The Greater Joining.
Tapes: ISBN 0-933291-80-9 • #T30 • 8 tapes $48

JESUS: The Manifestation of the Holy Spirit.
Tapes: ISBN 0-933291-81-7 • #T31 • 5 tapes $30

THE LAWS OF CHAOS: Our War with God.
Tapes: ISBN 0-933291-82-5 • #T32 • 12 tapes $72

"THERE MUST BE ANOTHER WAY."
Tapes: ISBN 0-933291-83-3 • #T33 • 1 tape $6
Available also in German:
ES MUSS EINEN ANDEREN WEG GEBEN

THE METAPHYSICS OF SEPARATION AND FORGIVENESS.
Tapes: ISBN 0-933291-84-1 • #T34 • 1 tape $6

Available also in German:
DIE METAPHYSIK DER TRENNUNG UND VERGEBUNG

THE WORKBOOK OF *A COURSE IN MIRACLES*:® Its Place in the Curriculum –
Theory and Practice.
Tapes: ISBN 0-933291-85-X • #T35 • 8 tapes $48

MAKING THE HOLY SPIRIT SPECIAL: The Arrogance of the Ego.
Tapes: ISBN 0-933291-86-8 • #T36 • 7 tapes $42

THE MEANING OF JUDGMENT.
Tapes: ISBN 0-933291-87-6 • #T37 • 1 tape $6

THE WEB OF SPECIALNESS.
Tapes: ISBN 0-933291-88-4 • #T38 • 12 tapes $72

DUALITY AS METAPHOR IN *A COURSE IN MIRACLES*®
Tapes: ISBN 0-933291-89-2 • #T39 • 8 tapes $48

RULES FOR DECISION.
Tapes: ISBN 0-933291-90-6 • #T40 • 8 tapes $48

I WANT THE PEACE OF GOD.
Tapes: ISBN 0-933291-91-4 • #T41 • 1 tape $6
Available also in German:
ICH WILL DEN FRIEDEN GOTTES

FORGIVING JESUS: "Stranger on the Road."
Tapes: ISBN 0-933291-92-2 • #T42 • 2 tapes $10

THE BIBLE FROM THE PERSPECTIVE OF *A COURSE IN MIRACLES*.®
Kenneth and Gloria Wapnick.
Tapes: ISBN 0-933291-93-0 • #T43 • 6 tapes $36

THE THEOLOGY OF *A COURSE IN MIRACLES*® Kenneth and Gloria Wapnick.
Tapes: ISBN 0-933291-94-9 • #T44 • 2 tapes $10

THE INHERITANCE OF GOD'S SON. Kenneth and Gloria Wapnick.
Tapes: ISBN 0-933291-95-7 • #T45 • 2 tapes $10

THE SIGN OF CHRISTMAS IS A STAR. Kenneth and Gloria Wapnick.
Tapes: ISBN 0-933291-96-5 • #T46 • 2 tapes $10

THE HOLY CHRIST IS BORN IN ME TODAY. Kenneth and Gloria Wapnick.
Tapes: ISBN 0-933291-97-3 • #T47 • 2 tapes $10

FROM TIME TO TIMELESSNESS.
Tapes: ISBN 0-933291-49-3 • #T48 • 1 tape $6

CLIMBING THE LADDER HOME.
Tapes: ISBN 0-933291-48-5 • #T49 • 5 tapes $30

HOW WILL THE WORLD END?
Tapes: ISBN 0-933291-47-7 • #T50 • 2 tapes $10

THE IMPORTANCE OF JESUS.
Tapes: ISBN 0-933291-46-9 • #T51 • 2 tapes $10

LEARNING FROM THE HOLY SPIRIT: A Commentary on Lesson 193:
"All things are lessons God would have me learn."
Tapes: ISBN 0-933291-46-0 • #T52 • 2 tapes $10

THE MEANING OF FORGIVENESS.
Tapes: ISBN 0-933291-44-2 • #T53 • 2 tapes $10
CDs: ISBN 1-59142-106-3 • #CD53 • 2 CDs $15

THE KINDNESS OF HEALING.
Tapes: ISBN 0-933291-43-4 • #T54 • 1 tape $6
CD: ISBN 1-59142-115-2 • #CD54 • 2 CDs $15

THE GIFT OF THE EGO: FEAR • THE GIFT OF GOD: LOVE.
Tapes: ISBN 0-933291-42-6 • #T55 • 8 tapes $48

THE EXPERIENCE OF *A COURSE IN MIRACLES*®. A Commentary on
"Development of Trust" (manual for teachers).
Tapes: ISBN 0-933291- 41-8 • #T56 • 8 tapes $48

SEPARATION AND FORGIVENESS: The Four Splits and Their Undoing.
Tapes: ISBN 0-933291-40-X • #T57 • 7 tapes $42

THE WORKBOOK LESSONS OF *A COURSE IN MIRACLES*®:
Tapes:
Vol. I • ISBN 0-933291-38-8 • #T58-1 • 8 tapes $32
Vol. II • ISBN 0-933291-32-9 • #T58-2 • 10 tapes $40
Vol. III • ISBN 0-933291-33-7 • #T58-3 • 11 tapes $44
Vol. IV • ISBN 0-933291-34-5 • #T58-4 • 8 tapes $32
Vol. V • ISBN 0-933291-35-3 • #T58-5 • 8 tapes $32
Vol. VI • ISBN 0-933291-36-1 • #T58-6 • 10 tapes $40
CDs:
Vol. I • ISBN 1-59142-120-9 • #CD58-1 • 7 discs $40
Vol. II • ISBN 1-59142-121-7 • #CD58-2 • 5 discs $30
Vol. III • ISBN 1-59142-122-5 • #CD58-3 • 5 discs $30
Vol. IV • ISBN 1-59142-123-3 • #CD58-4 • 12 discs $65
Vol. V • ISBN 1-59142-124-1 • #CD58-5 • 8 discs $45
Vol. VI • ISBN 1-59142-125-X • #CD58-6 • 9 discs $50
Vol. VII • ISBN 1-59142-126-8 • #CD58-7 • 10 discs $55

THE QUIET ANSWER: Asking the Holy Spirit.
Tapes: ISBN 0-933291-37-X • #T59 • 3 tapes $18

THE OBSTACLES TO PEACE.
Tapes: ISBN 0-933291-31-0 • #T60 • 8 tapes $48

CLASSES ON THE TEXT OF *A COURSE IN MIRACLES*®:
Tapes:
Vol. I • ISBN 1-59142-000-8 • #T61-1 • 8 tapes $32
Vol. II • ISBN 1-59142-001-6 • #T61-2 • 8 tapes $32
Vol. III • ISBN 1-59142-002-4 • #T61-3 • 8 tapes $32
Vol. IV • ISBN 1-59142-003-2 • #T61-4 • 8 tapes $32
Vol. V • ISBN 1-59142-004-0 • #T61-5 • 8 tapes $32
Vol. VI • ISBN 1-59142-005-9 • #T61-6 • 8 tapes $32
Vol. VII • ISBN 1-59142-006-7 • #T61-7 • 8 tapes $32
Vol. VIII • ISBN 1-59142-007-5 • #T61-8 • 8 tapes $32
CDs:
Vol. I • ISBN 1-59142-059-8 • #CD61-1 • 8 tapes $32
Vol. II • ISBN 1-59142-060-1 • #CD61-2 • 8 tapes $32
Vol. III • ISBN 1-59142-061-X • #CD61-3 • 8 tapes $32
Vol. IV • ISBN 1-59142-062-8 • #CD61-4 • 8 tapes $32
Vol. V • ISBN 1-59142-063-6 • #CD61-5 • 8 tapes $32
Vol. VI • ISBN 1-59142-064-4 • #CD61-6 • 8 tapes $32
Vol. VII • ISBN 1-59142-065-2 • #CD61-7 • 8 tapes $32
Vol. VIII • ISBN 1-59142-066-0 • #CD61-8 • 8 tapes $32
See also #V12-in. through V12-31 in Video Tapes section.

THE MEANING OF THE HOLY INSTANT.
Tapes: ISBN 1-59142-011-3 • #T62 • 2 tapes $10
See also #V9 in Video Tapes section.

FROM DARKNESS TO LIGHT.
Tapes: ISBN 1-59142-014-8 • #T63 • 4 tapes $20
See also #V16 in Video Tapes section.

THE PATHWAY OF FORGIVENESS.
Tapes: ISBN 1-59142-008-3• #T64 • 4 tapes $20
See also #V7 in Video Tapes section.

LOVE AND BE SILENT: King Lear, Defenselessness, and *A Course in Miracles.*®
Tapes: ISBN 1-59142-016-4 • #T65 • 4 tapes $20
See also #V11 in Video Tapes section.

JESUS: Symbol and Reality.
Tapes: ISBN 1-59142-017-2 • #T66 • 4 tapes $20
See also #V17 in Video Tapes section.

LIVING *A COURSE IN MIRACLES*®.
Tapes: ISBN 1-59142-018-0 • #T67 • 4 tapes $20
See also #V8 in Video Tapes section.

SPECIAL RELATIONSHIPS: The Home of Guilt.
Tapes: ISBN 1-59142-019-9 • #T68 • 4 tapes $20
See also #V10 in Video Tapes section.

DREAMING THE DREAM.
Tapes: ISBN 1-59142-020-2 • #T69 • 4 tapes $20
See also #V18 in Video Tapes section.

THE COMPASSION OF THE MIRACLE.
Tapes: ISBN 1-59142-021-0 • #T70 • 4 tapes $20
See also #V19 in Video Tapes section.

APPROACHING *A COURSE IN MIRACLES*®: A Commentary on Lesson 188:
"The peace of God is shining in me now."
Tapes: ISBN 1-59142-056-3 • #T71 • 1 tape $5

AN OVERVIEW OF *A COURSE IN MIRACLES*®.
Tapes: ISBN 1-59142-057-1 • #T72 • 1 tape $6

THE TIME MACHINE.
Tapes: ISBN 1-59142-058-X • #T73 • 4 tapes $20
See also #V14 in Video Tapes section.

FORGIVENESS AND THE END OF TIME.
Tapes: ISBN 1-59142-073-3 • #T74 • 4 tapes $20
See also #V15 in Video Tapes section.

HEALING THE DREAM OF SICKNESS.
Tapes: ISBN 1-59142-074-1 • #T75 • 4 tapes $20
See also #V20 in Video Tapes section.

THE CHANGELESS DWELLING PLACE.
Tapes: ISBN 1-59142-075-X • #T76 • 4 tapes $20
See also #V21 in Video Tapes section.

TO BE OR NOT TO BE: Hamlet, Death, and *A Course in Miracles.*®
Tapes: ISBN 1-59142-076-8 • #T77 • 4 tapes $20
See also #V22 in Video Tapes section.

FORM vs. CONTENT: Sex and Money.
Tapes: ISBN 1-59142-078-4 • #T78 • 4 tapes $20
See also #V23 in Video Tapes section.

THE PRODIGAL SON.
Tapes: ISBN 1-59142-082-2 • #T79 • 4 tapes $20
See also #V24 in Video Tapes section.

RETURNING HOME.
Tapes: ISBN 1-59142-083-0 • #T80 • 4 tapes $20

JUSTICE RETURNED TO LOVE.
Tapes: ISBN 1-59142-084-9 • #T81 • 4 tapes $20
See also #V13 in Video Tapes section.

THE PROBLEM OF EVIL
Tapes: ISBN 1-59142-096-2 • #T82 • 4 tapes $20
See also #V25 in Video Tapes section.

CLASSES ON THE MANUAL FOR TEACHERS OF *A COURSE IN MIRACLES*®
Tapes:
Vol. 1 • ISBN 1-59142-097-0 • #T83-1 • 10 tapes • $40
Vol. 2 • ISBN 1-59142-098-9 • #T83-2 • 10 tapes • $40
CDs:
Vol. 1 • ISBN 1-59142-107-1 • #CD83-1 • 10 CDs • $55
Vol. 2 • ISBN 1-59142-108-X • #CD83-2 • 10 CDs • $55
See also #V26-1 through #V26-10 in the Video Tapes section.

THE QUALITY OF MERCY
Tapes: ISBN 1-59142-100-4 • #T84 • 4 tapes $20
See also #V27 in Video Tapes section.

A TALE TOLD BY AN IDIOT: Macbeth, Guilt, and *A Course in Miracles.*®
Tapes: ISBN 1-59142-101-2 • #T85 • 4 tapes $20
See also #V28 in Video Tapes section.

THE JOURNEY: From the Ego Self to the True Self.
Tapes: ISBN 1-59142-104-7 • #T86 • 12 tapes $60
CDs: ISBN 1-59142-103-9 • #CD86 • 16 CDs $85

LIVING IN THE WORLD: Prison or Classroom.
Tapes: ISBN 1-59142-110-1 • #T87 • 8 tapes $40
CDs: ISBN 1-59142-105-5 • #CD87 • 8 CDs $45

HEALING: Hearing the Melody.
Tapes: ISBN 1-59142-111-X • #T88 • 4 tapes $20
CDs: ISBN 1-59142-109-8 • #CD88 • 4 CDs $25
See also #V29 in the Video Tapes section.

DECIDING FOR GOD.
Tapes: ISBN 1-59142-114-4 • #T89 • 2 tapes $10
CDs: ISBN 1-59142-113-6 • #CD89 • 2 CDs $15

LOVING NOT WISELY BUT TOO WELL: Othello, Specialness and *A Course in Miracles.*®
Tapes: ISBN 1-59142-117-9 • #T90 • 4 tapes $20
CDs: ISBN 1-59142-117-9 • #CD90 • 4 CDs $25
See also #V29 in the Video Tapes section.

JESUS: Light in the Dream.
Tapes: ISBN 1-59142-119-5 • #T91 • 2 tapes $10
CDs: ISBN 1-59142-118-7 • #CD91 • 2 CDs $15

LETTING GO OF JUDGMENT: Entering the Stately Calm Within.
Tapes: ISBN 1-59142-128-4 • #T92 • 4 tapes $20
CDs: ISBN 1-59142-127-6 • #CD92 • 3 CDs $20

PSYCHOTHERAPY: PURPOSE, PROCESS AND PRACTICE: A Commentary on the Pamphlet.
Tapes: ISBN 1-59142-130-6 • #T93 • 8 tapes $40
CDs: ISBN 1-59142-129-2 • #CD93 • 8 CDs $45

JESUS: "The Ancient Love."
Tapes: ISBN 1-59142-135-7 • #T94 • 4 tapes $20
CDs: ISBN 1-59142-134-9 • #CD94 • 4 CDs $25

ESCAPE FROM LOVE: Dissociating *A Course in Miracles.*®
Tapes: ISBN 1-59142-138-1 • #T95 • 2 tapes $10
CDs: ISBN 1-59142-137-3 • #CD95 • 2 CDs $15

WALKING WITH JESUS
Tapes: ISBN 1-59142-140-3 • #T96 • 2 tapes $10
CDs: ISBN 1-59142-139-X • #CD96 • 3 CDs $20

JESUS: "Bright Stranger."
Tapes: ISBN 1-59142-145-4 • #T97 • 4 tapes $20
CDs: ISBN 1-59142-143-8 • #CD97 • 4 CDs $25

See next page for ordering information

Ordering Information

For orders *in the continental U.S. only*, please add $6.00 for the first item, and $1.00 for each additional item, for shipping and handling.

For orders to *all other countries* (SURFACE MAIL), and to *Alaska, Hawaii*, and *Puerto Rico* (FIRST CLASS MAIL), please add $6.00 for the first item and $2.00 for each additional item.

California State residents please add local sales tax.

VISA, MasterCard, Discover, American Express accepted.

Order from:

Foundation for *A Course in Miracles*®
Dept. B
41397 Buecking Drive
Temecula, CA 92590
(951) 296-6261 • FAX (951) 296-5455
or

visit our Web site at *www.facim.org*

* * * * *

A COURSE IN MIRACLES and other scribed material
may be ordered from:

Foundation for Inner Peace
P.O. Box 598
Mill Valley, CA 94942
(415) 388-2060

A COURSE IN MIRACLES, Second edition (hardcover): $35
A COURSE IN MIRACLES, Second edition (softcover): $30
A COURSE IN MIRACLES, Complete edition (paperback): $20
PSYCHOTHERAPY: PURPOSE, PROCESS AND PRACTICE: $6
THE SONG OF PRAYER: PRAYER, FORGIVENESS, HEALING: $6
THE GIFTS OF GOD: $21
CONCORDANCE OF *A COURSE IN MIRACLES*: $49.95

Additional copies of this set may be ordered from:

Foundation for *A Course in Miracles*®
Dept. B
41397 Buecking Drive
Temecula, CA 92590

Send a check or money order (in US funds only) for $25.00 plus shipping: please see preceding page for shipping charges.

Foundation for A Course in Miracles®
Dept. B
41397 Buecking Drive
Temecula, CA 92590

☐ I am interested in receiving a newsletter

☐ I am interested in receiving a catalog of publications

☐ I am interested in receiving a schedule of workshops and classes

☐ Place me on your mailing list to receive your catalog and quarterly newsletter

PLEASE PRINT NEATLY

Name _____

Address _____
_____

City, State, Zip _____